Take Your Life to the Next Level

How to Think, Act and Win

Jamie Lewis
www.CeilingCrusher.com

Please consult a licensed professional before attempting any techniques outlined in this book.

IBSN 978-1-955078-01-6 (eBook)

ISBN 978-1-955078-00-9 (print)

ISBN 978-1-955078-02-3 (audio)

First Edition: *March 2021*

Produced by iii Sides Publishing

www.iiiSides.com

"If you CHANGE the way you look at THINGS, the THINGS you look at will CHANGE"

.... Wayne Dyer ....

This book is dedicated to

My loving wife Carrie,

Four beautiful children:

Hannah, Kaden, Casen, Denton

and my precious

first grandchild, Bash.

Contents

Introduction

The ancient Greek philosopher, Heraclitus, couldn't have said it better thousands of years ago when he famously proclaimed that, "Change is the only constant there is in life." We seem completely ignorant to these essential words of wisdom that can be applied to any component in our lives—the one piece of advice that will open our eyes to understanding the ongoing metamorphosis we experience as human beings. Those who do not see life this way would most likely regard Heraclitus as an ancient simpleton who wore a bed sheet and ate dates and grapes for breakfast, lunch, and dinner. If only they were to look around them, they would see that proof of his theory is as evident as the change of the seasons. People seem to prefer surroundings characterized by the constant, most probably because change can be uncomfortable and uncertain, and it doesn't always lead to happy endings. However, to deny the natural flux in ourselves and our environments is to go against our very nature. Some seem to understand this better than others, and on top of that, they handle the flux more efficiently than those who choose to hold on to a constant that will inevitably be no more. The question is, what do these individuals understand that others don't, and what is this ability that seemingly helps them to understand almost everything around them?

In the early part of the 20th century, a man named Alfred Binet developed intelligence tests that were considered, at that point, revolutionary, as the tests were a very successful tool used to measure and predict a student's academic success and level of achievement. The tests were very successful and accurate regarding the type of intelligence that they were designed for; however, they were created to test a type of intelligence that was required for success in the Western school system, but not necessarily for success when entering the real world. There is no doubt that scoring high on a test that follows Alfred Binet's design will prove significantly valuable in life, but this doesn't mean that it is the only form of intelligence in existence or the only type of intelligence required for success in life. However, this method was the mainstream approach to intelligence throughout the 20th century, despite signs of EI's recognition sticking out its head here and there in the '50s.

We are now more informed about how diverse the human brain actually is, and not only that, but how challenging it can be to navigate society and make a successful living. As knowledge is power, and we now know about the existence of emotional intelligence, testing our own abilities is possible as is utilizing strategies to develop and apply techniques to improve different aspects of life and to achieve success using a not new, but newly-discovered or identified ability.

In this book, you will discover the complexity of emotional intelligence, and will be reassured that it is an attainable skill. For some, it comes naturally and for others, it doesn't, just like any other human traits that may become manifest in behavior among individuals. This book is an in-depth guide to emotional intelligence which includes a detailed explanation of its research and academic components as well as how to apply the techniques to different aspects of your life to become a happier, healthier, and more successful individual.

Chapter 1

EI, EQ, and E-Everything Else

Emotional Intelligence has always been a part of the human mind, active on different levels as required throughout human existence, but it was first officially identified and proclaimed as being prominent in the 1990s. The existence of emotional intelligence means that the human mind is not only capable of cognitive intelligence, which we identify by the term IQ, but that there's another ability separate from logic and rational thinking called the EQ or *Emotional*

Quotient. This is the brain's level of emotional intelligence, which is relevant to social interaction, how an individual handles strong emotions, and how emotions are expressed. Since the 'discovery' of emotional intelligence, it has been widely discussed and is proclaimed to be a vital life skill. So, when exactly did humanity suddenly need to know about emotional intelligence to improve themselves and their position in society? Alternatively, did humanity build themselves into a society that requires an advanced level of emotional intelligence for survival and success? Either way, the importance of knowing and mastering the art of EI today is undeniable. Here's how it began as part of an academic dissertation during the late 1900s.

The History and Research of Emotional Intelligence

Descartes' famous quote *cogito ergo sum* or "I think, therefore I am." has been enthusiastically changed to "I feel, therefore I am." by prominent Indian scholar and psychologist, Amit Abraham, to illustrate the relevance and importance of emotional intelligence and the official discovery thereof. There is one general definition accepted by society and a more scientifically-oriented one among scholars. The widespread definition of emotional intelligence is much like the one provided above; it is the ability to control one's emotions and to understand interpersonal relationships by handling them justly and with empathy. The scientific approach provides more specific details and defines emotional intelligence as "using emotions for enhanced thinking and to have the ability to reason about emotions." This includes a person's ability to identify and grasp emotions, to access and develop emotions that are conducive for thought, and to have the ability to regulate emotions in such a way that it promotes emotional and intellectual growth within the person.

Emotional intelligence is not only about understanding and using your own emotions, but also about being able to accurately read the emotions of others and using them constructively. One example of using emotional intelligence is as a constructive tool in conflict resolution. This skill can help you to achieve goals and overcome challenges that would have been much harder or even impossible if you'd used only traditional IQ, which is actually only useful to a certain extent. This is because an individual's emotional quotient has to do with the understanding and identification of productive uses of emotion and how to use it to, for example, relieve stress, communicate in a way that is effective in a specific situation (like with conflict resolution), and to empathize with those around them. By using emotions in these ways, one can overcome obstacles in life much easier and reach goals quicker with less stress. People around us can cause stress because misunderstandings can cause stress. Not reading others accurately can cause stress and problems if an incorrect assessment of someone leads to trust.

I know I said that the concept of emotional intelligence is a child of the '90s, but its conception actually occurred in the '50s. Quite a long incubation process, I must say; or maybe it was just a matter of waiting for the right opportunity. The first time a flicker of this concept sparked to life was in 1953 when famous literary scholar, Dorothy van Ghent, was reading the Jane Austen novel *Pride and Prejudice,* and making notes in her book about the high levels of emotional intelligence of some of the characters in the story. Then, in 1966, which was during a period notorious for various types of drug testing, the German psychoanalyst, Barbara Leuner, hypothesized that LSD could possibly help women with a naturally low emotional intelligence, which she attributed to being separated at an early or premature stage from their mothers. Although these two women referred to emotional intelligence, the individual who coined the term was Wayne Payne in his dissertation completed in 1986. In his discussion, he argued that emotional awareness is a component crucial to the development of children.

Payne's dissertation opened a new door in psychological studies, and academics burst through with zeal to observe, argue, and discuss emotional intelligence. The first "theory of EI" was introduced by Mayer and Salovey in two journal articles written in 1990 in which they provide the first suggestion of how EI can be measured along with their own formulation of the concept. One can say that this made EI an official determination in an era where the IQ was revered for its ability to predict an individual's cognitive abilities. During the '90s, society was still busy debating where IQ comes from and whether there is a genetic link; constituting the basic nature versus nurture debate about the origin of the IQ. This was about to change during the mid-'90s when a new thinker and pioneer stepped onto the EI stage.

Daniel Goleman and EQ

Daniel Goleman, a science reporter, took particular interest in the two groundbreaking articles published in 1990 by Mayer and Salovey that were based on Payne's dissertation about emotional intelligence. He decided to develop another perspective on emotional intelligence, suggesting how it can be used as a tool to achieve success in life. His perception of emotional intelligence was different and more complex than Payne's, and he used the term "emotional intelligence" to unite several different scientific strands that had previously been regarded as separate. For example, Goleman gave depth to the research of emotional intelligence by combining the research of neuroscience in an era when this research field was still in its primitive state.

In 1995, Goleman published his book *Emotional Intelligence: Why It Can Matter More Than IQ*. Interestingly enough, even though Mayer and Salovey's articles published in 1990 were seen as groundbreaking at that time, there were still many health practitioners who have never come across any material discussing emotional intelligence or heard about emotional intelligence within five years of it being published. Thus, Goleman's book took many people completely by surprise. While the articles remained relatively unknown except to the tightly-knit academic community, Goleman's book became a bestseller and EQ quickly became the shortened global term for emotional intelligence. Goleman's hypothesis is that emotional intelligence is twice as important as cognitive intelligence when it comes to predicting someone's success in their career. One of the focal points where EQ is applied is in business and employee relations, but its implementation in school curricula has also been researched and implemented to a wide extent (Counselling Connection, 2016).

How Is EQ Tested?

Goleman initially developed a model of EQ that is performance-based to ultimately assess employees' emotional intelligence. The purpose is to identify where a specific individual's areas of improvement are and where their strengths lie. The model consists of five separate components:

1. An individual's *self-awareness* is tested as the first component. If an individual has a high level of emotional intelligence, they will not only understand how they impact others, but they will also be comfortable with their own emotions and thoughts. The reason why these elements of self-awareness show a high level of emotional intelligence is because acceptance and understanding one's own emotions is the first step to conquering emotional issues.

2. The second part of the model is testing *self-regulation*. Self-regulation has to do with a person's ability to control their impulses and manage strong emotions. For example, a person with a lower emotional intelligence would make rash decisions and act on impulse, while a person with higher emotional intelligence would take a moment to assess what's going on inside them. Making rash decisions can lead to relationship damage and other mistakes that will lead to regret.

3. Strong *internal motivation* is a sign of high levels of emotional intelligence. This, however, doesn't refer to motivation towards achieving material or monetary goals, but rather developing a passion for what you do or what you want to do in life. Understanding the importance of this internal motivation will lead to long-term motivation as well as clear decision-making.

4. Having highly developed *social skills* is a clear sign of emotional intelligence. This level of social skills doesn't equate to just being friendly for the heck of it, but it refers to social interaction with a purpose. This purpose can be to build healthy relationships, which an individual can benefit from personally.

5. Finally, but just as important, there is *empathy*. Empathy is a dead giveaway when it comes to whether someone has a high level of emotional intelligence. Empathy is the ability to understand your own emotions and also understanding the emotions of others and reacting appropriately and with intelligence. Reacting with intelligence means that your reaction to someone else's emotions should have a positive or proactive effect rather than cause unnecessary conflict, and this is achieved by emotionally intelligent individuals by understanding the emotions of others (Accipio, 2018).

After the development of this five-point model, Goleman revised and refined it by developing a four-point model in 2000. These four points can also be seen as a deconstruction of the five points into four quadrants. Goleman's argument remains that cognitive intelligence can be used to measure and contribute to business success, but not without the presence of emotional intelligence.

The Four Quadrants

The four quadrants are closely related to leadership and leadership skills and, if you've ever read a self-help book about becoming a better manager, chances are that these quadrants were mentioned and/or discussed in depth. Although EQ is mostly associated with business management and leadership, it is related to all aspects of our lives, whenever we form a relationship with someone or come into contact with another individual. Goleman explains that emotional intelligence consists of four fundamental capabilities: *Self-awareness, self-management, social awareness,* and *social skill.* Some of these quadrants overlap with the five-point model and some are new. Each quadrant consists of smaller components that explain the bigger concept and how it should be interpreted and applied if you want to compare yourself to these standards in your own capacity.

1. The first quadrant is self-awareness. From this term, we already understand that those who have a high level of self-awareness have the ability to understand their own emotions and also the emotions of others. There are three important sub-points that should be considered in the context of the main quadrant to grasp how broad the concept is and which abilities are important components of self-awareness:

- Firstly, one should not only be aware of emotional awareness per se, but emotional self-awareness. Emotional awareness is a new development from the five-point system with the aim of making the definition of emotional intelligence more specific and easier to understand. Emotional awareness is specifically the ability to read and understand one's own emotions and to also understand their impact on other aspects of one's life like different types of relationships, performance at work, and activities that involve human interaction in some way.

- Then, self-awareness also relates to one's ability to perform accurate self-assessment, which is, straightforwardly, a realistic evaluation of one's limitations and strengths. In other words, if you have a high level of self-awareness, your idea of what you can and cannot do will not be based on low self-esteem, but on a rational perception of your abilities.

- This ability to rationally assess your own self-awareness comes from another inherent component of self-awareness, which is healthy self-confidence. In this context, you can look at healthy self-confidence as a positive and strong sense of self-worth and a strong self-image.

These three sub-points are the main components of the first quadrant, and it should not be considered without also considering these three points thoughtfully along with their definitions.

2. The second quadrant is self-management, which I think we can all agree on is a crucial life skill. However, to do it efficiently, requires a high level of emotional intelligence. It also has quite a few sub-components—6 of them—which shows that self-management in itself may be more complicated than we think. It's not just waking up in the morning, knowing what you're going to do, and doing it. However, Goleman provides some great insights and a heads-up for those of us who want to master the art of self-management to achieve success in life:

    - There is no doubt that if you want to self-manage effectively, you need to practice self-control. Most of us struggle with self-control, whether it's going on a diet, trying to implement a new lifestyle change, or making changes to our behavior to improve our relationships. However, what Goleman means by self-control in this context is being able to control impulses and negative or disruptive emotions instead of acting on them. For example, acting out immediately when you're feeling angry instead of taking a moment to assess how your behavior may affect the situation you're in and others involved in the long term. Individuals with a high emotional intelligence find this form of self-control naturally easier and don't necessarily have to do so much mindful practicing to master the skill. Goleman's more specific definition actually applies to all of the examples mentioned above. What's your take on this? Do you often act out on impulses or take a step back to think first?

- Another integral component of self-management is trustworthiness and integrity. So, what does this mean? Do you stay true to yourself and also true to others? For true self-management, you'll find that both are important. Consistently displaying a character of integrity and upholding honesty as a core value is part of effective self-management that will lead you to success, wherever you plan to go.

- To take initiative means that you can identify and are always ready to take on new opportunities. This adds a proactive component to effective self-management and it means that you are not passively practicing self-managing, but doing it actively and with intention. Taking initiative in terms of self-management means that you are managing your career, relationships, and life in such a way that you are always on the lookout for improvement. You are ultimately managing while always seeking opportunities to move forward in life.

- The next sub-component is closely related to taking initiative, and this is adaptability. If you have a high emotional intelligence level, then you may also understand that taking initiative and being adaptable are mutually inclusive. I mean, if you are not prepared to make changes, how are you going to take initiative, which is a basic form of change? Apart from adaptability being closely related to change, it can sometimes be hard to do, especially if you have to adapt to a new situation that you don't really like. That's where emotional intelligence comes in. If you have that EQ, you'll find a way to cope, adapt, and before you know it, you'll be moving on, looking for new ways to improve your life.

- Have I mentioned conscientiousness yet? Conscientiousness is a sub-definition of self-management as it means, in this context, to have the ability to manage your responsibilities and yourself as an individual. Consider conscientiousness not only as a sub-component but, also as a refined definition of this quadrant.

- The final sub-component is one that indicates the high standards of an individual with emotional intelligence. It is called achievement orientation. Achievement orientation is an individual's drive to meet their own level of excellence, and their personal standards are likely to be pretty high. An individual with a high level of emotional intelligence is probably aware that they may have to adapt and will leave space for new initiatives when setting their internal standards. However, it is not only this that defines achievement orientation, but also their inner drive to reach their goals.

3. The Social Awareness quadrant seems like a logical deconstructive component from the original five components. In this context, good social awareness means being observant of others' emotional states and needs and knowing how to respond in a productive way:

    - Empathy is the first sub-component of social awareness and it is a crucial skill for forming and maintaining meaningful relationships. Goleman defines empathy as the ability to sense the emotions of others, being able to understand their perspective, and 'get' where they're coming from, and being genuinely and actively interested in their concerns. If you have these abilities, chances are that you have strong relationships in your life. Being genuinely interested in other peoples' lives is not always on our to-do lists, but it can be a rewarding venture.

- Social awareness is also linked to organizational awareness. This is the ability to read the flows and currents of the organizational aspects of life and use them to construct your own decision networks and ways to navigate through life's politics. In short, it's knowing how things work around you, regarding relationship structures whether at work or at home. It's the ability to see the mechanics in social and emotional components as they form part of human life and the way they're put together. Does it sound complicated? It may be a level up from other sub-components discussed under the quadrants—it's a big-picture thing.
- The final sub-component under social awareness is service orientation. Service orientation is usually interpreted from a business or service provider-client perspective, but it can actually be applied to

any type of relationship. It's the ability to recognize and, based on that recognition, being able to meet the needs of others. This means that, to some extent, you need to be fine-tuned to the emotions of others, which will most likely show you their needs. There are several ways to identify and recognize these needs, which we will be focusing on in-depth a bit later on.

4. The final quadrant, social skill, ends the discussion of the quadrants with a bang. The social skill quadrant has the greatest number of sub-components that need to be considered in order to understand the quadrant in its entirety:

    - The first subcomponent of having social skills is having visionary leadership. If you think about it, people who have a sense of visionary leadership usually have very strong social skills as well. Demonstrating visionary leadership means being able to inspire and take charge with a strong vision that draws others naturally.

    - Next, we have influence. Social skills cannot be social skills without the ability to influence others. This does not mean that you have to influence others to meet your own selfish needs or to do bad things; however, if you want to reach your goals in life or help other people, influence can be a powerful tool. It is also a natural skill of those who have high emotional intelligence.

- Along with influence comes developing others. The one is largely dependent on the other as others will not have the drive or will to develop if they are not influenced in some way. In the context of developing others, influence can be seen as providing guidance and feedback to help build their abilities and skills. These are also examples of using influence for a good cause.

- When working with people, one component that is unavoidable is conflict. Whether it involves you or happens in close proximity to you, if you have the skills, you'll be able to deflate such a situation, conduct dispute resolution, and help the relevant parties to look for a win-win solution without causing any overreaction or emotional issues.

- Here we are at communication, which sits at the heart of social skills. Communication is not only what you say to people, but how good a listener you are. A good communicator sends clear and unambiguous messages and listens intently in order to do so. These messages are also finely tuned in on the receiver's emotional state. Communication is not only a crucial social skill, but it is one of the sub-components that forms the center around which all the others revolve.

- If you have strong social skills, it will most likely be easy for you to be a catalyst for change. As we discussed earlier, adaptation is one of your strong points, so helping others to do the same by using effective communication is something you do naturally. Being a catalyst for change can also link to developing others; if people around you need to adapt to a changing environment, you can not only lead them in this change, but influence them to make the change more bearable.

- An individual who is socially skilled has the ability to form and nurture bonds with others, which means that they are good at cultivating and maintaining not only individual relationships, but also a network of relationships. Building bonds is thus an important sub-component.

- The final sub-component is strongly associated with building bonds as well as being an individual skill. The last part of discussing social skills involves being good with teamwork and collaboration. This doesn't necessarily mean that you are a good team member; it focuses more on your ability to promote cooperation within a team and to act as a strong team builder. In other words, this sub-component should be seen as a leadership skill as well as the ability to collaborate (Stareva, 2016).

When you compare the first five-point model to the second, deconstructed four-quadrant model, the four-quadrant concept provides more valuable insight about emotional intelligence and how the components fit together. There are four main points instead of five, but they are each well-developed, giving the reader a clear idea about the nature of each quadrant, the skills that go with them, and how these skills relate to everyday life.

The Importance of Understanding Emotional Intelligence

It is not only important to understand emotional intelligence, but also beneficial to understand how important emotional intelligence is in everyday life. In all aspects of life, we as humans encounter stress, emotional highs and lows, interactions with other individuals, whether we like them or not, and possible opportunities that we can take to move forward, improve our lives, and achieve success, whatever way we choose to define it. To navigate through all of these obstacles smoothly, emotional intelligence is the ultimate tool.

Apart from all this, cognitive intelligence can bring you far in life as it gives you the ability to develop a range of complicated skills that are required in today's job market. However, having a high IQ cannot give you insight into how to live a fulfilling life. For example, mathematical skills can get you a high-paying job in the financial sector, but does that mean that you'll automatically have rewarding and satisfying relationships with those around you and understand how the world works from a social or emotional perspective? Look at it this way: It's your IQ that'll essentially get you that approved college application, but you need some solid EQ to deal with concurrent issues like stress management, emotional roller coasters that come with the social aspects of college life, and becoming a stronger and more resilient human being.

Emotional intelligence affects you from a young age, and the most important aspects of your life that have been noted to suffer from a lack of EQ includes your academic performance or your performance at work, your physical health, your relationships and mental health, and your level of social intelligence.

First, applying developed emotional intelligence in the workplace will not only help you to deal with work-related stress, but it will also help you to cultivate healthy relationships with coworkers and will give you the ability to motivate and lead others. Companies commonly let applicants for positions in management take an emotional intelligence test as part of the application process to measure their EQ, which they now know will have a profound effect on their ability to effectively do their job.

Your physical health is closely related to your ability to handle and process stress and stressful situations. Unregulated stress and anxiety can subsequently lead to high blood pressure, a low immune function, acceleration of the aging process, and a higher risk for strokes and heart attacks.

Being aware of your EQ is also crucial in situations that affect your mental health. When you look at all the aspects of a person's character that are relevant in the four quadrants, emotional resilience is definitely present. If you are not emotionally resilient, and again, not able to deal well with stress, your mental health can suffer, and there is potential for you to develop depression. Uncontrolled emotions combined with loneliness can also lead to further mental health complications if you are not able to steer the situation properly.

The effect of emotional intelligence on relationships should, on the one hand, go without saying, but on the other hand, there is so much to say. Having EQ just enables you to understand your partner much better, understand communication processes much better, and deal with conflict much better. And, you can do this because you have the ability to understand, contextualize, and control your own emotions. I barely touched on the subject here—we'll discuss relationships in-depth later and give you the ultimate inside scoop.

Finally, underlining all of these aspects in your life and the fundamental reason why emotional intelligence is important to understand is that it opens the door to understanding the world of social interaction, its intricacies, its politics, and how to navigate social situations like a pro.

Chapter 2

Emotional Intelligence and Mindset

EQ alone is a powerful tool. However, if you want to make it work for you and you come across especially difficult obstacles in your life, there are other tools that you can use to help you to understand them contextually, see the bigger picture, and climb those mountains you never thought you could. Emotional intelligence is an inherent quality in some individuals, but a constructive way to apply your mind to support EQ when the going gets tough is by developing a positive and constructive mindset. A constructive mindset is more commonly known as a 'growth' mindset and can be linked in many ways to a person's level of emotional intelligence as well as their ability to improve or develop EQ.

The Definition of a Growth Mindset

The concept of a growth mindset, which is now widely known among practicing psychologists and scholars, was coined by Dr. Carol Dweck, a psychologist herself. The concept is specifically characterized by the fundamental belief that a person's intelligence, as well as their abilities, can be developed and improved, depending on a person's own perception of their mindset. The opposite of a growth mindset is a fixed mindset, where an individual would, instead of having the perception that they can develop, improve, or learn, stagnate intellectually because of the fixed state of their mindset.

Dr. Carol Dweck and the Growth Versus Fixed Mindset

What makes the discovery of a growth versus fixed mindset so interesting is that it began with a psychologist, Carol Dweck, and her interest in failure and children's attitude about failure. Considering the explosion of positivity that came from this interest, one can see the irony in the situation and also in Dweck's growth mindset about her achievements. Dweck's interest was tweaked over three decades ago as she observed students and how they dealt with setbacks, no matter how small. Sometimes, a person's reaction to the smallest and most insignificant setback (or so it seems) is the most telling. Dweck decided to make the research official, and she spent her time studying thousands of children and their behavior and reactions related to their environment. There appeared to be two clear poles that separated the way that children handled situations, both based on a mindset. Dweck called one the fixed mindset as it was set in its ways and unwilling to develop or show a strong will to grow. She called the other the growth mindset as it had the opposite characteristics. Both mindsets are fundamentally based on a person's underlying beliefs and perceptions about their own intelligence and learning. To Dweck's surprise, students who believe they can learn quicker and more efficiently actually do, in comparison to students who believe they can't or that they have only a certain capacity to learn.

Now, decades later, neuroscience also has a finger in the research pie, and consequently, we can now understand the growth mindset from a neurological/physiological context. The research was conducted specifically on brain plasticity, and results from this research indicated that the connections between neurons that form networks, can be changed over time by changing both behavior and experience. However, these neural changes happen the quickest when stimulated by practice. With such practice, the brain starts growing new connections, strengthening the productive ones that exist, and also creates a form of insulation that speeds up inter-neural impulses.

During this same period that neurological research was conducted, researchers started linking achievement and mindset. Believing that you can be smarter can actually make you smarter, and the capability of change that comes from belief also shows that it is possible for an individual to make a life-changing transformation from a fixed mindset to a growth mindset. If you are unsure about your own mindset, there is a quiz you can take online that will point you in the right direction (Mindset Works, 2017).

Understanding both mindsets will enable you to understand the growth mindset to a better extent, so here's an illustration of different situations and how they will be approached and handled by a fixed mindset versus a growth mindset:

- In terms of capabilities and abilities, a fixed mindset would take a "use what you have" approach, while a growth mindset would take a "my abilities can be improved and developed" approach.

- When approached from the aspect of achievement, the fixed mindset will hold tightly onto the abilities and capabilities it has, where the growth mindset will naturally have a broader perspective that not only includes their capabilities but an "anything is possible" attitude. This perception alone helps someone with a growth mindset to improve and develop their capabilities where someone with a fixed mindset will stay in the same position until they are forced to develop or change.

- If you face a challenge with a fixed mindset, you will aim to overcome it, if you think it's possible, by using the skills you have. However, if you have a growth mindset, you will implement fierce determination that naturally develops character and skills in order to achieve your goals.

- Risk is a very unpleasant experience for someone who has a fixed mindset. The person who has a growth mindset has a significantly increased tolerance for risk and may even see it as opportunity.

- A very interesting way of looking at the two mindsets is through a lens of focus. The approaches of individuals who have differing mindsets find that interpretations can't be more different. When it comes to focusing, the fixed mindset prioritizes performance, while the growth mindset uses it primarily for learning and improvement, which will ironically, also lead to high performance and success that may even exceed the performance level of a fixed mindset.

- Finally, feedback is just as fascinating of a lens to look through, and I'm sure we've all met both types of individuals who respond to feedback either with a fixed or a growth mindset. The interesting part is, which one we've encountered more. The fixed mindset doesn't like feedback very much and can respond defensively and critically. The growth mindset, on the other hand, embraces feedback and views it as an opportunity to learn as their response is rooted in curiosity.

The Link Between Mindset and Emotional Intelligence

Because emotional intelligence can be defined as a set of abilities regarding emotions, which include a person's abilities to understand their own and the emotions of others, to express emotions in an effective and conducive manner, and to manage emotions effectively, note that research has also indicated that emotions can be a guide to our own behavior and way of thinking. This ascertains a definite link between emotional intelligence and a growth mindset. Positive emotions, which are closely related to emotional intelligence, help to broaden our thinking skills and build conducive behaviors like paying attention, asking questions that show interest, and interact more with an aim to explore and learn. Behaviors like these are commonly linked with emotional intelligence, and they are also essential elements of a growth mindset. In contrast, negative emotions tend to limit our interest in what's happening around us and consequently, will not inspire engagement or further exploration. Negative emotions like these will also cause a person to react defensively when being critiqued or being offended easily; therefore, negative emotions, which are not commonly associated with a growth mindset, are linked to a fixed mindset.

When you think about it, emotional self-awareness is the component of emotional intelligence that we use to monitor our own emotional state, which can lead to a person developing either a growth or a fixed mindset, depending on their level and developmental status of emotional self-awareness. Our ability to manage our own emotions is the component of emotional intelligence that enables us to turn our negative thoughts into positive ones and, of course, the other way around. This emotional self-management makes it possible for a person to remain in a growth mindset even in difficult times by retaining perspective while it would have been easy to lose perspective and slip into a fixed mindset. Then, emotional awareness is the component of emotional intelligence that gives us the ability to identify a fixed or growth mindset in others, which will help us to determine how to approach, interact, and motivate them. Having emotional intelligence means having the ability to positively influence others and also to help them make this crucial mind shift. Here are some useful examples that can paint a clear picture of how finely intertwined emotional intelligence and the mindset actually are:

EQ INFLUENCE	GROWTH MINDSET	FIXED MINDSET
SELF AWARENESS	*Present in the moment* • Reflects on own feelings • Awareness of the impact own thoughts can have on emotions • Awareness of impact emotions can have on interactions with others	*Disconnected/Absent* • Indifference towards own feelings • Reduced awareness of the impact of own thoughts • Reduced awareness of impact emotions has on others
AWARENESS OF OTHERS	*Empathetic* • Being able to accurately identify the feelings of others • Read body language efficiently • Being able to view situations from others' perspectives • Adjust well socially	*Insensitive* • Not understanding the feelings of others well • Not paying attention or identifying the importance of body language • Focused on own perspective • Struggles to adjust

AUTHENTICITY	*Genuine* • Sharing feelings with others • Being tactful • Choosing an appropriate time to share feelings and information • Being able to facilitate conversations effectively • Helping others by encouraging them to express themselves	*Untrustworthy* • Prefer to hide feelings • Not always aware of tact and how to apply it • Not mindful of when to share information • A diminished ability to facilitate a conversation • Would rather avoid motivating others
EMOTIONAL REASONING	*Wide-ranging* • Reflects on own feelings when making a decision • Reaching out to others for their input • Approach a situation from multiple perspectives from the get-go • A natural awareness for biases in a decision-making process	*Limited* • Decision-making skills are more limited • Relies on own thoughts and ideas instead of including the opinions of others • Likely to have a mono-perspective • Likely to overlook biases in a decision-making process

SELF MANAGEMENT	*Resilient* • Effective response in situations that can cause stress • Can adapt easily to changing circumstance • Takes criticism well and finds it useful • Focused on self-improvement	*Temperamental* • Doesn't deal very well with stress • Resists natural adaptive processes and change • Defensive and offended by criticism and responds negatively • Mentally and emotionally stagnant
INFLUENCE	*Empowering* • Aims to offer support for others • Helps others to respond positively to stressful situations • Always aims to create a positive environment • Try to positively influence others	*Indifferent* • Is not focused on others' needs • Struggles to respond to stressful situations themselves • Indifferent to the environment • No drive to influence others

The table above shows us how closely a growth mindset is linked to the main components of emotional intelligence and how far removed the fixed mindset is from a high EQ (Palmer, 2018). The behavioral components in the growth mindset column correspond almost exactly to the traits of someone who has a high level of emotional intelligence. If one can develop a growth mindset after having a fixed mindset, then surely one can learn how to increase one's emotional intelligence. What other skills can one use to drive that EQ and growth mindset into the clouds? Some are seen as sub-components of either emotional intelligence or the growth mindset or even both, but they deserve an individual approach and discussion to supercharge our knowledge and know our game from every possible angle.

Proactivity

A little proactivity goes a long way. Very much like the growth-fixed mindset, proactivity can be defined and easily understood if contrasted with its less appealing counterpart, which is reactivity. Proactivity fundamentally translates into taking responsibility for the things that happen in your life instead of sitting back and watching them happen. It sounds complicated because sometimes, all we can do is stand back and watch things happen because we feel like they are completely out of our control. So, how do you take control? Being proactive in everything that you do is a very effective strategy for just that. Proactivity is an ongoing mental process that involves considering options and alternatives, anticipating events and how to effectively deal with them, and making decisions based on accurately identifying future events. Proactivity is a self-created and self-maintained influence that comes from the inside while reactivity is a demonstration of taking action in accordance with occurrences in life that are controlled by outside forces.

A basic example of proactivity would be avoiding a mistake after you've made it once before. Anticipating the situation the second time around and taking precautions to avoid a mishap is a proactive behavior. However, you don't need to make a mistake to become more proactive. By assessing your surroundings and analyzing future outcomes rationally, you can also benefit from proactive behavior by acting in a preventive manner. Another example of proactiveness is being aware of what your short and long-term goals are and reviewing them on a regular basis (Sáez, 2020).

Proactivity is defined by the Merriam-Webster dictionary as anticipating future problems, changes, or needs. If you're anticipating these issues, then you're most likely to be prepared for them when they arrive and ready to deal with them either before they have a negative effect on you or by making the necessary adjustments to fit into a new environment or situation. This idea reminds me very much of one of EQ's four quadrants; specifically, the self-management quadrant. Being proactive definitely opens one up to change and helps to prevent unnecessary or unpleasant events by identifying them in an anticipatory fashion. Proactivity means that you're not only looking at what's on your urgent list, but also at what's on your important list before these items become urgent and possibly problematic.

Another interesting way to look at proactivity is to see the difference between doing things and getting things done. Which one of these indicates genuine progress? A proactive individual is constantly moving forward while a reactive individual is content with staying where they are until unforeseen (by them) circumstances push them into a new direction. This is why proactivity will always outperform reactivity. The most prominent characteristic of proactive individuals is that they are, first and foremost, disciplined. Proactive behavior does not come without being tested by your environment, so it requires self-discipline to maintain a proactive attitude. As your circumstances can drag you back into a routine of reactivity, being mindful of your proactive attitude and applying self-discipline is crucial. This is how one becomes a successful proactive individual.

A great tip to always keep in mind for maintaining a proactive attitude is that you cannot always control your circumstances, but you can control the way that you handle them, prepare for them, and respond to them. Keep in mind that the world around you will always tilt toward reactivity. The more stress you encounter, the more resilience toward reactivity you will have to show. Once you are able to achieve this, you will find it to be an incredibly freeing experience.

Another valuable tip, that you can tattoo on your chest if you like, is that success is never the result of circumstance; it is the result of a proactive response to circumstance. Look at yourself in the mirror every morning and know that you are in control of your own destiny. The following tips can help you to build a resilient and overall proactive approach, so let's look at the ideas, and while you're reading the points below, try to envision applying them along with characteristics of a high EQ:

1. The best way to maintain a high level of self-discipline is to have a good reason, and that should be a good reason for you, not anyone else. Aspects like self-awareness and emotional reasoning can help you to identify a good reason and will also help you to understand why you are making certain

decisions. It's even been proven by research that, if you have a clear goal in your mind like a 100-meter sprinter can see the finish line before them, then your chances to stay on track and reach your goal will be significantly higher.

2. This is an oldie, but it's worth its imaginary weight in gold. Get rid of that terrible procrastination habit. From a rational point of view, all procrastination does is create stress, stress, and more stress. And, even though an individual with a high EQ is able to handle stress effectively, would they purposefully create stressful situations for themselves? Underneath the tattoo on your chest about success, add a tattoo that says, "I am too smart to be a procrastinator." Consider using a different font for this tattoo, just in case you get confused, as tattoos don't usually have any end punctuation. If procrastination is your Achilles heel as it is for many others, there are some activities you can do mentally to get rid of this nasty habit. For example:

    - Create a hyper-realistic picture in your mind of how great you'll feel when you've completed whatever task you're busy procrastinating. The sensation you imagine should be vivid, bright, and almost tangible. Taste it! Now, do it.

- Tell a lot of people when you're going to be finished with whatever you're busy with. In this way, you will be creating a form of accountability if you have none other than yourself.

- Break it up into steps, and do it step-by-step, unless what you're procrastinating is as simple as going to buy milk. In this case, you can't break up the task, and I can't even think of a way to do that at this point.

- After you've completed the first step, reward yourself. The only reward that's off-limits is procrastination.

3. This may sound counterproductive, but in a lot of cases, proactivity means saying no. Understanding why requires some emotional intelligence. An emotionally intelligent individual knows how to look after themselves and navigate emotionally through stressful situations. A proactive person can identify unimportant or unessential tasks or

obligations scheduled for a specific time. Thus, if you are faced with one of these obligations and the only contribution it will make in your life at this point is to cause extra stress, the proactive approach is to say no. By combining proactivity and emotional intelligence, you will be able to identify when you can say no to a task or obligation without it being harmful to another party or having negative consequences. There's nothing wrong with taking control of your own time. Instead of feeling guilty for not donating all of your time to the needs of others, understand that proactively giving yourself some downtime is a way to keep yourself mentally healthy. A great alternative approach to uttering this scary two-letter word is to set boundaries.

Proactive thinkers know that, even if things are going well, there's always room for improvement. It's the ultimate tool that leads to the ultimate manifestation of the growth mindset (Ewers, 2017).

Positivity

Positivity is a word that has been used *ad nauseam* in speeches, books, conversations with your friends, and in the media. Phrases like "Just be positive, everything will work out" or "look on the bright side" are advice we've probably all heard before. Even the patronizing "It's not that bad." An individual with a high level of emotional intelligence is not likely to tell you "it's not that bad" because it's actually a counterproductive response when someone seeks advice or comfort. I am not criticizing someone's genuine effort to be positive, but positivity may be understood incorrectly and therefore be ineffective in most people's lives.

What is positivity? Additionally, what does it mean to think or feel positive? Generally, society views positivity as a collection of short-lived experiences that are uncomplicated and that don't require the same amount of scrutiny or research as negative emotions like anxiety and depression. However, positive emotions are closely intertwined with emotional intelligence, which means it is not simple or uncomplicated at all. It is an extremely powerful ability that has several important effects on our emotional and mental well-being. For starters, positive emotions have the ability to broaden an individual's thought-action repertoire, which means our thinking and attention is being broadened and, in turn, a greater variety of positive thoughts and emotions. These thoughts translate into action. For example, interest and happiness or joy stimulates creativity, the ability to identify opportunities, to develop genuine relationships with those around you, and to be open-minded and flexible.

Next, positive emotions are strong and complex enough to actually undo negative emotions. By deliberately focusing on positive emotions, and experiencing them while you are going through a negative emotional experience, can prevent the negativity from lingering. Even a mild experience of happiness or some contentment can have a radical effect on a stressful or depressing situation. Another great benefit you can get from positive emotions is that they literally enhance your strength and resilience. Actions like general enjoyment, contentment, the upkeep of meaningful relationships, and even playfulness make you a more resilient human being. Being positive means that you can infuse negative events with positivity or use positivity as a coping mechanism. This approach links with a high level of emotional intelligence, as clinging to negativity when things are not going so well could make the situation worse, even though it's much easier to maintain negativity when the going gets tough. Ultimately, positivity will help you to not only cope, but also to bounce back quicker after experiencing difficulties in your life. Experiencing positivity will cause an upward spiral in your personal and professional development as well as in your relationships. This ultimately means that your outlook and emotions will promote your becoming a better version of yourself.

Just like the yin cannot exist without the yang, positivity cannot exist without negativity, or at least, it will not be definable. This also means that negativity also contributes to positivity in some ways, and researchers have discovered the ideal positive/negative ratio is 3:1 as this supports healthy development and thriving. However, anything below this ratio; for example, 2:2 or even 2:1, will not have the same effect and will ultimately steer in a negative direction. Too much positivity is also dangerous as a ratio of 8:1 and above can lead to counterproductive results or effects. Here are the secrets of negativity that all positive and emotionally intelligent individuals know and that we can all benefit from knowing:

- Suffering and having negative experiences can lead to a positive outcome if handled with a positive outlook. One can gain wisdom and new insight from a bad experience; it all depends on how it is handled and dealt with.

- Negative emotions can help you to reconnect with yourself before rediscovering positivity.

- Negative experiences like trauma or a personal crisis can cause a fundamental and positive change in a person's character or personality.

- Negative emotions can bring us to a place of depth within ourselves that we haven't experienced before, which can unlock strength and resilience. Wisdom is often gained more from negative than positive experiences because the individual having the experience is using it for self-improvement.

- Coping with negative situations in your life or experiencing them can lead to better social and emotional skills as it can help an individual to understand and practice empathy, modesty, care, and considering issues from a moral perspective (Boniwell, 2008).

When talking about positivity and emotional intelligence in the same sentence, positivity is interpreted as a tool that individuals with high EQs use to improve communication skills, to improve their level of resilience, and manage positive and negative emotions effectively and intelligently by taking from the negative what they can to improve themselves and become smarter human beings. For people with high emotional intelligence, the positive is not always

100% positive and it's not just the outcome that matters. It's the process of turning from negative to positive, the wisdom such a process can provide, and the elation of knowing that you've learned something new about yourself. That's emotionally intelligent positivity.

Reading Body Language Accurately

Reading body language is a natural and inherent skill for some, but not everyone is as tuned into this silent, but effective, language. This may be because they don't see any particular value in reading body language, that they may think there is more value in verbal communication than the non-verbal type, or it may just be that an individual is more withdrawn and not the observant type. Nevertheless, once you start focusing on non-verbal communication, you'll find that different individuals tend to do the same things with their arms, hands, eyes, lips, and posture in specific situations, and these postures signal hidden information about what they are thinking or feeling. In order to be empathetic or to influence others in an effective manner, you need to know what they are not telling you.

When you become aware of how important emotional intelligence is, you will also realize that it's not only important to focus on the messages that you get from others, but you also need to be super-aware of your own body language. This is because, whether you believe in the effects of body language or not, your body language makes a subconscious impression on those around you. When looking at facts, Dr. Albert Mehrabian, who is the current leading expert on body language, can tell us a few things from studies that have been conducted specifically on non-verbal communication. You may be astonished to find that only 7% of communication is conveyed through words. However, a word comes with a voice, and the vocal element, which includes elements like tonality and upward and downward slants in speech, contributes a far larger component, which is 38%. Vocal elements are not classified as verbal communication, but as nonverbal because, while they voice words, the words themselves are not in question. Then, the type of body language we usually deem as conventional body language, which is the ways that we subconsciously use our bodies to send messages, sends out the largest portion of a message to others; a whopping 55% (Fletcher, 2015). Are you still a doubter? I think it's at least useful to know the basics of body language as, according to experts, it plays such a large role in how messages are conveyed from one individual to another.

When you look at the four quadrants of EQ and what they entail, you'll notice that all of them are closely related to the concept of understanding body language. Let's refresh:

- Self-awareness: Understanding yourself so that you can understand others.
- Self-management: Being able to regulate your emotions and being open to change
- Social awareness: Understanding and reading people and situations accurately.
- Relationship management: Intelligently interacting with and understanding others.

Now, let's combine the element of body language to indicate its importance and how it has been present in these components for all of this time:

- Self-awareness: This includes being mindful of your body's posture, your tone of voice, and other nonverbal components, ensuring that you deliver your message in a way that fits the context of the situation. For example, if you have to let your neighbor know that their husband passed away, chances are you're not going to shout at them with your arms crossed over your chest.

- Self-management: Self-management involves paying close attention to your own body language and how it changes as the environment around you changes.

- Social awareness is about understanding the body language of those around you. For example, if someone is sitting with their head in their hands, chances are that they are not very happy at that moment.

- Relationship management is closely linked to self-awareness as it is the ability to constructively change and adjust your body language to different situations.

In your normal, day-to-day life, there are specific mannerisms and customs that can help you to read the body language of those around you, which will enable you to read a social situation, whether at work or at home, with more insight.

1. You can tell a lot from another person by shaking their hand, and at the same time, you can teach yourself how to use a handshake to make the right impression. The impression of a handshake is definitely underrated. That being said, a proper

handshake doesn't only include shaking hands—it includes other factors such as body proximity and eye contact. Let's start by focusing on the shake first. Society typically thinks that a firm handshake signals a solid and confident individual, while a limp handshake gives the impression that an individual lacks confidence and may not be interested in interacting with the other shaker. You also get the type of person who crushes all the bones in your hand. If you're meeting someone for the first time and they try to break your hand, this can signal that they may be a bit on the aggressive side or that they have already identified you as competition and they are trying to establish their dominance and make their mark. If someone shakes your hand, but they don't make eye contact, that is an immediate red flag that can signal anything from disinterest, disdain, or dislike. On the other hand, if they try to laser beam into your soul and hold eye contact for longer than what feels natural, the individual may be trying to make up for feeling insecure or it may just be the accessory that goes with the bone-crusher handshake. The best method for a solid handshake is to show no judgment towards the other party. Just exude confidence and be friendly and genuine. Give them a friendly look in the eyes, give a brief and firm shake, and you're all done. If they don't do the same, you will know what may lie behind their actions.

2. Personal space is an interesting component of body language because many individuals will not realize that they are expressing a form of non-verbal communication until the person next to them tells them that they're moving in too close to their personal space. However, personal space is actually crucial, and it can be complicated because the accepted or frowned-upon spaces between individuals differ from culture to culture. The amount of personal space that you give someone else also depends on your relationship with this individual. How would you feel if a complete stranger stood very close to you in line at the grocery store? Would you feel the same way if it was your partner standing that close to you? I'd say that, if you can smell the person's shampoo or deodorant, you are definitely too close. But, keep in mind that you don't want to stand too far away, as this may create the impression that you lack confidence.

3. When someone is talking to you, do you turn your whole body in their direction to face them, or do you tend to turn sideways and cross your arms? There is a big difference in the message that you are sending to this person which can affect their perception of you. It's not just your head that needs to face someone when you are having a conversation. Sure, sometimes when you're sitting in your car and your neighbor walks over to chat to you, it's not necessary to try and do the impossible, but if your body is in a position to face the other person and it doesn't, it can send messages ranging from disinterest to disrespect for the person themself or for what they are saying. If your boss calls you in to talk to you, for example, it is important to send a subconscious message of respect by turning your whole body towards them. Posture is an easy type of body language to read and it makes a lasting impression. Before we move on to the next point, how would one define the correct way to face someone? Your foot placement should mirror the person you are talking to and your shoulders should be, if possible, parallel to that person. Show that you are engaged in the conversation by leaning ever so slightly forward

while looking the person in the eye. Showing someone that you are giving them your undivided attention is a sign of respect.

4. There are other elements regarding posture that are important in non-verbal communication. If you sit up straight and stand up with good back posture when you are talking, you are signaling a position of authority. Slouching is a serious no-no if you are having an important conversation, whether it be with your partner, your children, or your boss. When you or someone you are talking to slouches, it indicates a lack of intention or that you or they are not taking what is being said seriously. It can also translate as a form of disrespect that the person may hold toward you that they are unknowingly showing. Teenagers often slouch because they tend to battle with self-esteem issues, and low self-esteem is also a reason why people may slouch when interacting with others. In this context, slouching can be seen as a way for an individual to hide their body as they are not comfortable with themselves. You can figure out which type of sloucher you are talking to by looking at their eyes, at other signs of engagement, and how they respond when you are interacting with them. For example,

someone who lacks respect may avoid meaningful eye contact and there may be no quality of their responses, while someone who is merely struggling with self-esteem issues is likely to still listen, but have that issue of feeling physically uncomfortable that they are also battling with.

5. Eye contact can be a dead giveaway to a person's intentions and feelings. It's hard to explain to someone else as people are not generally tuned into non-verbal cues. For example, you cannot say to someone, "I know she's lying. I saw it in her eyes!" However, the eyes are an excellent place to look for signs of dishonesty, guilt, and other deceptive emotions. If you are speaking to someone about a serious issue and they avoid making eye contact, it is definitely a reason to suspect that they're hiding something. When evaluating a person's eye contact during a conversation, it is important to consider the context of the conversation itself, as a less formal or less serious conversation will not necessarily indicate guilt if the individual is not making eye contact. It could also be a case of insecurity or a lack of confidence. The person may find you intimidating, or they may have a different cultural background that has other customs related

to eye contact. Being emotionally intelligent means that you are observant enough to be able to consider all of these factors before coming to a conclusion. If you suspect that it is a cultural difference, try to avoid seeming forceful with your approach and keep your body language open and accepting when you communicate. If you need to break eye contact for a moment, it's best to glance sideways instead of downwards as this may signal a lack of self-esteem.

6. Has anyone ever told you they can read your face like a book? Alternatively, do you have a poker face? Whichever it is, keeping to your authentic self and not forcing expressions is the best way to go. Keeping that in mind, it's not a good idea to blatantly show expressions of disgust, disdain, or dislike. If you are emotionally intelligent, these expressions will not cross your facial features often because your mind will thoroughly process a situation that may lead to such a response and will instead lead to a more appropriate response that is well-adjusted and constructive toward your surroundings. People do tend to make the funniest facial expressions and not notice it, though. Smiling is always the best way to go. However, if you are the more serious type and your smile tends to

unintentionally manifest in a grimace or a sneer, you can show that warmth through your eyes by making meaningful eye contact (Deutschendorf, 2019).

Your Body Language Toolkit

Body language should always be read in the context in which it is expressed for it to be constructive and accurate. This toolkit provides basic and general meanings for gestures and postures that we often observe in the people around us; however, keep in mind that they should not be interpreted in isolation.

Confidence:

- Prolonged and solid eye contact.
- An open positioning of the arms.
- The face is not tense and shows relaxed muscles.
- The movement of the upper limbs is wide and relaxed.
- There is a sense of purpose in the individual's style of walking.
- Firm (but not too firm) handshake.

Uncertain or Anxious

- Facial muscles are tense and tightened.

- Fists can be clenched.
- Unable to hold solid eye contact.
- Movements of the upper limbs are more erratic.
- Arms are more likely to be folded across the chest in a protective stance.
- Weaker handshake.
- Aimless or undecided walking.

Not Paying Attention or Bored

- Not looking up/keeping the head down.
- Eyes are fixed on something else, causing little to no eye contact.
- A slumped posture.
- Eyes can be glazed over.
- Hands are busy. For example, fidgeting, doodling or drumming fingers on a table.

Defensive

- Also little to no eye contact; eyes may be downcast and brooding.
- Arms are crossed over the chest in a defensive manner.
- The individual will show little emotion or a neutral facial expression.

- The body will be turned away, especially the upper body.
- Hands will be kept close to the body and gestures will remain small and protective.

Considering Prior to Responding

- The individual may break eye contact until they re-engage with a response. At this point, they will make eye contact again.
- Fingers can likely be touching the chin in a resting position.
- The individual's hand can be placed on their cheek.
- The individual can be focusing on something else in their surroundings without their eyes glazing over (Fletcher, 2015).

Take a Step Back

In order to successfully implement proactivity, positivity, a growth mindset, and accurately reading the body language of others and fine-tuning your own, there is one thing that you always need to do, and that is to take a step back. All of these components are brilliant for managing your environment, improving relationships, and achieving your goals, but a critical skill that goes with all of them is to avoid acting impulsively, looking at a situation from an isolated perspective, and/or acting before all dimensions of a situation have been considered. This ability is what makes emotional intelligence the form of art that it is and what leads individuals who practice it using this approach to be so successful. Now that you know how all you need to know about EQ, let's apply it to life, relationships, and how to achieve ongoing success.

Chapter 3

Emotional Intelligence in Relationships

Relationships are a core part of our lives, and most of us can say that we have good ones and bad ones. Some of us are talented socializers while others are unsure about how to interact with others. Social skills and smart socializing start with emotional intelligence. In this chapter, we're looking at different social situations (even the dreaded ones) and how to rid yourself of social anxiety, to start enjoying the social side of life.

Emotional Intelligence for Social Situations

Strong social skills can take you far in life because effectively communicating with others is the key to most successes and happiness in life. Social skills are a component of emotional intelligence and, as you will see throughout this book, it forms a major part of every chapter. Emotional intelligence is a person's way of perceiving and observing, but it usually outwardly manifests in communicating, and that's why communication is so important. Many consider social skills to be the final piece of the EQ 'jigsaw' This statement is based on the motivation that emotional intelligence initially starts with developing a comprehension for your own emotions or self-awareness, and then their management, which is self-regulation, used for achieving goals (self-motivation). Then, once you have acquired these abilities, you move on to understanding the emotions of others in the form of empathy, which leads to the ability to influence them—ultimately known as social skills.

Even though social skills are seen as the last (singular) piece of the emotional intelligence jigsaw, they are multifaceted and comprise several elements. Social skills, from the perspective of emotional intelligence, can be divided into the following components:

- Leadership Skills
- Communication Skills
- Conflict Management Skills
- Influencing or Persuasion Skills
- Change Management Skills
- Building Rapport
- Team-Working Skills

Leadership skills share an unbreakable bond with emotional intelligence. A leader has the ability to lead because of other components that they possess due to a high EQ, such as persuasive skills and good communication skills. A good leader, for example, will not have a need to be in an official leadership position or require the title of leader in order to act as a leader or to fill a leadership role; this may be because, for this type of person, leadership comes naturally. They understand that leaders are not only required in official positions, but that they have an ability to identify where these roles are required. A good leader will also hold those around them accountable while providing the necessary support and guidance. One can only hold others accountable if one leads by example, so this is an essential skill of good leadership. Finally, a leader, hence the name, should lead others in a specific direction and therefore, has the ability to develop a vision and communicate this vision to others. Considering these characteristics and the official leaders you are aware of in present day and in history, who do you think were or are good leaders?

One cannot place enough emphasis on communication skills. Effective communication can be tricky because it's not only about talking, as one would think; there are other important skills involved in effective communication on a high level. Other skills that are involved in effective and intelligent communication are good listening skills, being able to clarify and avoid miscommunication between parties, and a willingness to apply reflection to the process. Good communicators take into account the point of view of the individuals with whom they are communicating, and they are prepared to do problem-solving just as much as they are to receive positive information. They also have the ability to read signs, whether verbal or nonverbal, from the other party and to react appropriately. Good communicators know that, if they are confronted with an issue, it's better to solve it as soon as possible and not leave it for later as the communication process could only become more complicated.

Conflict management goes hand-in-hand with communication and listening skills are specifically important here. Conflict management is part of effective communication because, if an issue can be resolved as soon as possible, additional complex issues and disagreements can be avoided. An individual with a high level of emotional intelligence understands that conflict management requires active listening as well as diplomacy and the use of tact when communicating. Using these tools makes it easier to ease tensions to diffuse a situation. Someone with good conflict management skills also has the ability to tactfully expose disagreements or conflicts so that they can be proactively resolved. They encourage open and honest discussions as they know that this is the best way to avoid tension and unnecessary conflict.

When you think of influencing skills and a persuasive individual, does it remind you of a sleazy door-to-door salesman who keeps your front door open with their foot or that telesales consultant who just won't allow you to say no when trying to sell you insurance? Those are examples of what we are not discussing relative to persuasion and influence. It really is an art, and what most people who have this skill as a job requirement don't realize, is that you have to invest time and energy in the relationship with the person who you want to influence. Influence, if used in the correct way, is not meant to pull a cloak over someone's eyes or to get something out of them without making any effort. In true high EQ-style, one needs to, just like you would with any other aspect of life, invest in the person and your relationship with them in order to persuade or influence. Good influencers and persuaders have the ability to read emotional vibes going back and forth between them and another individual and they use these vibes to guide them toward communicating in a way that appeases the other person.

Regarding change management skills, a change manager is someone who is an expert at self-regulating and who is not afraid of change. They also use their leadership and interpersonal skills to be the first to initiate change, and they have the ability to do this without making it frightening or unpleasant for other individuals who would be affected. A change manager has the intelligence to identify when a change needs to occur and they will proactively make the process as smooth as possible by removing obstacles that may alienate or cause stress to those involved. This is a skill tailor-made for a leader, as such an individual will not only initiate the change, but will also be its foremost example.

Building rapport is an essential social skill if your work requires networking or interacting with clients. It is a process of building and consequently maintaining relationships with other people to keep them in good shape. Interestingly enough, if you have good rapport-building skills, this will also benefit your long-term relationships. The core motivations behind these skills are the desire to know more about others, and being interested in others in general.

Collaboration is something we need to do in all aspects of life; at work, in relationships, and if we have a family. Even if you are someone who prefers to work alone, having the ability to collaborate shows that you possess emotional intelligence. People who are good at team-working can improve the work of all team members and thus, the performance of the team as a whole. A good collaborator doesn't need to be in a leadership role either; they can fit in anywhere in the chain of command, using their skills to draw everyone together.

Now we know that social skills, which are categorized as only a singular component of emotional intelligence, are multidimensional in themselves to quite a large extent. Because of this, it is easy to identify an emotionally intelligent person through their social and interpersonal actions. However, emotional intelligence still begins with a thought (Skills You Need, 2011).

How Important Is Emotional Intelligence in My Relationship?

Relationships between individuals are in some ways constant and in other ways always in that infamous flux. An example of a constant is that your relationship keeps its status and will always be called a relationship. An example of flux is that you and your partner's wants and needs will most likely change over time as you develop as individuals and as a couple. The closer you are to someone and the more of your life you share with them, the more you will realize these changes and understand how they can affect the stability of your relationship. Emotional intelligence is a crucial skill for steering and maintaining healthy relationships because it provides a finely-tuned ability to notice and contextually understand changes and fluctuations within a relationship. If you want your relationship to outlast situations of conflict that may not have been necessary in the first place, learning about using your EQ and improving your EQ to avoid these situations can lead to long-lasting relationship success. It can also provide benefits such as enjoying a rewarding experience of going through life with your closest partner beside you, and learning how to grow together effectively.

Just as there is more than one type of relationship, the word 'love' also has different definitions, of which only one refers to romantic love. The different names for love originate from ancient Greek and Latin (but mostly Greek). Here are the ones most relevant to our discussion:

- *Storgē:* This type of love is most often connotated with a familial type of love, meaning that it refers to the love between parents and their children, but it can also refer to romantic love. This type of love is specifically described as a natural and effortless feeling of love that you can experience when you are close to someone who makes you feel good. Considering this definition, it makes sense that *storgē* would then both be used for family, parental, and romantic love as they all carry this element.

- *Philia:* The type of love that *philia* represents is a deep bond of friendship that automatically includes trust, being able to depend on one another, and companionship. It is, ultimately, a deeply-nurtured feeling of goodwill for another person, which, if you think about it, is a crucial component for a successful partnership.

- *Eros:* This is the quintessential element of romantic love. It represents a passionate, sexual, and intimate type of love between two people. *Eros* is the most accurate representation of what we see as a romantic relationship.

In relationships, emotional intelligence can be identified as both partners' abilities to be in touch with their own and with the emotions of their partners. Two crucial components of emotional intelligence are a person's capacity to show and experience empathy and their ability to use empathy to communicate constructively about their emotions. There are certain key points where emotionally intelligent couples may have a different and more constructive approach than other couples that makes their relationship more successful in the long run. Couples who share a high EQ also share a deep sense of friendship. They place each other's wants and needs high on their priority lists and therefore, they stay close friends and are able to cultivate a long-term relationship. They also share a sense of deep mutual respect and understand the importance of maintaining this crucial bond. Mutual respect links with a sense of admiration for each other and these partners appreciate each other's abilities, unique qualities, and achievements. This feeling is also physically expressed in verbal and nonverbal ways to cultivate an ongoing sense of appreciation and respect.

Couples who share the trait of high emotional intelligence tend to have a healthy approach to communication. This means that they don't argue when they are emotional, but instead, wait it out until they are more clear-headed before engaging in conversation. This reduces the chances of one or both partners saying hurtful things that they don't really mean or a sense of resentment developing from either side. They don't interrupt each other because they understand the importance of listening to each other's opinions in order to 'get' each other. When communicating, they will also only give criticism when needed and never with the intention to hurt or upset the other partner (Bisignano, 2018).

Using EQ in Intimate Relationships

Emotional intelligence gives each of us the opportunity to attain the love we want and need in our lives. Most people want commitment, mutual kindness and friendship, a physical or sexual connection, and openness from both parties for developing a deep level of caring. To achieve this level of satisfaction in a relationship requires a high level of emotional intelligence, and to make it specific to relationship improvement, there are points that one can focus on.

One of the characteristics of emotional awareness that we all know by now is emotional awareness. This characteristic or quality is important if you want to weed out the ones who are not going to last from the ones with genuine potential. Having a strong sense of emotional awareness gives you the ability to tell the difference within yourself and your then-partner between mere infatuation, lust, and long-term love. You may be interested in a long-term relationship, but if you can sense that your partner isn't, then is the relationship worth it? Will you be able to change your partner's views?

In intimate relationships, focusing on improving one's emotional intelligence can make a dramatic difference between being together and really wanting to be together forever. It teaches how to develop a manner of sensitivity that all partners are looking for in a significant other; we are all looking for someone who will understand and love us for who we are and accept those attributes that we perceive to be faulty within ourselves. Intimate relationships are harder to navigate because the partners are so close to each other that they are able to sense even the smallest shifts in the relationship's dynamics.

We have the potential to achieve the type of affection that we want, which includes intimacy, mutual kindness, real commitment, and emotional caring—all simply as a result of empathy. Empathy in an intimate relationship is our inherent ability to share emotional experiences. However, to reach and attain the level of romance that we want, we need to learn how to use all of the components of a high EQ. We need a sharp emotional awareness to see the difference between infatuation or lust and lasting love, we need the ability to accept so we can fix emotional issues that might damage a relationship if left to fester, and we need to develop a sense of alertness and active awareness to help us to identify what's working and what isn't.

Another ability characterized in emotional intelligence, that can save you a lot of conflict, is the ability to identify emotions that, if not dealt with immediately, can cause long-term harm. If one or both partners harbor feelings of unfair treatment or being dismissed or disrespected by the other, and these feelings are left to fester, they can have long-term damaging effects on the relationship. Nipping toxic emotions like these in the bud immediately with constructive communication will prevent further conflict or a sudden outburst of anger weeks of months later. If you have that level of EQ, you'll also get that gut feeling whether it's going to work or not. You'll know, so don't ignore it. Instead, be observant on the inside and in your surroundings and try to identify the reasons why you get this feeling if you don't already know.

These are examples of how EQ can help you to make the right choices at the beginning of a relationship while you have yet decided if you're going to commit. A great thing about EQ is that you don't need to be an expert when you're starting off in a relationship; the relationship itself can be a learning process for you if you know what the most important components of EQ are, and you actively keep yourself open to practicing them mentally. Growing your and your partner's EQ is the best thing you can do for your relationship as, surprisingly, this is the fifth element that lets the romance keep on blooming, makes you stronger as individuals and as a unit, and keeps the flame of excitement alive. Here are some of the most productive ways to start practicing emotional intelligence in your relationship:

1. One of the behaviors that causes the most problems in relationships is demonstrated when one partner seeks change while the other wants to avoid it.

Change is natural, and actively seeking change is a characteristic of emotional intelligence. Partners should not be afraid of change, as long as they reassure each other that they are in the relationship together and that they have each other's support. Resisting change is going to cause dissonance between partners, and the ability to understand change, being adaptable, and supporting change in each other are essential characteristics of emotional intelligence that will take relationships very far.

2. Here, we don't encounter only emotional intelligence, but a clear idea of the growth mindset. What I mean by this is that, in a relationship, one should view obstacles or challenges as opportunities and not as problems or issues. The keywords here are optimism and courage. The growth mindset meets obstacles with a sense of creativity and a positive outlook that strives to improve instead of simply solve or clear up. A high emotional intelligence frees you from traps that you would normally find yourself stepping into as you possess the ability to broaden your approach and your outlook. Being emotionally intelligent means that you can see obstacles as an opportunity to become closer to your partner, to learn new things

from your partner, and to become stronger as a unit.

3. When it comes to feelings, all couples, no matter how much they love each other, will have good and less good feelings about each other—you know, those things they do that can really grind on you. An emotionally intelligent approach would be to not resent your partner for the things that they find irritating or less appealing about you, but rather to accept you for who you are as an individual. Can you laugh or joke about a relationship flaw in a non-sarcastic way? This action shows acceptance of all of the cracks and chips in the relationship instead of trying to intellectualize every emotion and attempting to make it too perfect. There's no such thing as a perfect relationship, and high emotional intelligence imparts the understanding that the flaws are also there to be celebrated, even if it means you celebrate them by making them the butt of an inside joke.

4. Do you and your partner laugh together? You should. It takes the weight off of things when someone with a high level of intelligence is unable to clear the air. Laughing seems like such a simple

and child-like thing to do; however, don't underestimate its importance. We all have an inner child. Don't be shy to show yours.

The Three Gauges of Well-Being and EQ

The three gauges of well-being are manifestations in your body and mind that indicate a level of health. They are having mental clarity, feeling energized, and feeling loving towards others. When you are in a relationship and all three gauges of well-being are present, this is a good sign that the relationship has a bright future. However, this bright future is not going to build itself. The good news is that the three gauges are helpful tools that can help you to make accurate assumptions and choices in your romantic life. They are the ropes that one uses to learn about using and applying EQ in relationship decisions.

Emotional intelligence will always tell you that communication is the best route. You can use the three gauges of well-being to estimate if you are in a favorable mental state to have a constructive discussion with your partner. For example, feeling mentally clear is crucial when you want to have an open and honest discussion with your partner. If you are feeling mentally clouded, your judgment could be impaired by emotion. If you want to express how you feel, do it authentically. It is important to let your partner know how you feel and, even more importantly, in your unique, individual way. If you want your relationship to have a future, it is important for you to love each other for who you are. An emotionally intelligent person is a good listener. When your partner talks to you, keep your mind clear and be emotionally close to them to get the best understanding of their perspective.

A high EQ will give you the ability to understand why you should always be prepared to work on a relationship. This means that you should be prepared to put the work in when it's going well and especially when things go wrong. Constant work is what is going to keep the relationship moving forward. Work in terms of relationships includes listening skills, open and honest communication, unconditional support, and mutual understanding. If you keep working on your relationship, even if there is no prominent issue, you will reap the rewards when you suddenly experience one.

Remember that, when one makes a mistake in a relationship, whether it be due to a lack of judgment or a spur-of-the-moment decision that didn't turn out well, the worst thing you can do is to not admit to your mistake. You may encounter a situation where your partner thinks that you did something wrong or made a mistake, but you don't, and even then, you and your partner need to find a middle ground instead of having a "battle of who has made the most mistakes." Emotional intelligence teaches us that we need to look further at what can happen later if the problem is not dealt with quickly or at all. In this case, if one partner keeps on doing things that the other may find offensive or that are hurtful towards them, but refuses to apologize, then this short-sightedness can lead to serious relationship problems (Vader, 2019).

Dealing With a Low EQ Partner

There are several different scenarios when it comes to intimate relationships because every relationship is unique. For example, consider what could happen if one of you makes the choice to improve their emotional intelligence, but the partner doesn't want to or doesn't believe that emotional intelligence is really that effective. From the perspective of a partnership, it really is ideal if both partners commit to this development, which can be seen as an attempt to reach new heights, resolve relationship issues, and/or reach relationship goals. Moreover, even if you are both working toward becoming more emotionally intelligent, your progress will most likely not be similarly paced, possibly because one partner may have a larger capacity for developing emotional intelligence than the other. In cases like these, the partner who is developing faster or who is the only one focused on developing their EQ may, understandably, experience feelings of intense frustration and even disappointment. However, there are strategies that can be considered to effectively respond to a partner with a low EQ and who may not be a good listener and communicator. Don't lose hope yet.

- In a situation where you need to communicate with a partner who has a lower EQ than you do, a great strategy is to, as you usually would, consider their feelings, their perspective, and what they want to hear from you. Communicating your needs in their language may be your best bet at successful communication, even though it would have been easier if your partner were as emotionally intuitive as you were.

- Create a suitable environment where your partner will be more susceptible and open to communication and listening. For example, cook dinner, create a relaxing atmosphere, and do something that you know they enjoy so that they will open up more easily. If they are going to be uncomfortable from the beginning, whatever you want to discuss with them is going to be a lot harder because they are not prone to sensing your needs.

- Instead of just expressing yourself, make sure to include the words or a subtler version of "I feel," so that your partner gets the idea that what you are telling them is important and that it is more serious than just a casual conversation. Stay diplomatic and encouraging, but get your message across by being sensitive to their insecurities.

- There is always a chance that your partner will show a defensive reaction to this kind of approach. If this happens, acknowledge that you are aware of their concerns or insecurities by repeating it back to them. For example, you could say, "You feel like I'll not be spending enough time with you if I take this new job." By vocalizing it back to your partner, they will immediately understand that you get them and this can open up the path to a further discussion.

- After you've verbally acknowledged their concerns, use the "I feel" approach again without being too pushy or showing signs of frustration. Keep this up until your partner gives you the reaction or answer you want from them and you think it is now clear to them what your needs are (Vader, 2019).

Emotional Intelligence for Friends and Family Woes

Have you ever considered cutting all contact with a family member, your parents, a sibling, or a friend just for the sake of your sanity? This happens more often than you think. This may be due to conflict or unresolved issues that have been going on for years, and every time you see each other at a family gathering, it's dug up again and a fight ensues. If you think about this scenario, it's not very rational, especially since you've known these people for so long. You must have figured out what their strong and weak points are in terms of their personalities and whether they are likely to change at all. If they have bad habits they stick to, it doesn't mean that this needs to affect you in a negative way or that you have to respond impulsively every time you see them.

Because your friends and family with whom you have these relationships are not likely to change, you can change by controlling the effect they have on you. Emotional intelligence teaches us that we can determine and change our environments by using self-awareness, self-regulation, social skills, and empathy. Here are a few scenarios that you can consider to keep your relationships with family and friends cordial, and they may even improve from the effort.

Firstly, if you don't want your blood to start boiling unnecessarily, do not take anything they say, whether it is innocent or malicious, personally. It's difficult when hurtful comments come from a family member or a friend whom you've known your whole life, but if they are doing it to get a reaction out of you and you show no reaction, they are likely to stop doing it anyway. Emotional intelligence includes the ability to look at the world from another person's shoes, and by doing this, you may realize that what they say is coming from a place of insecurity or due to low self-esteem. Remember to take a step back. In a situation where you feel provoked, keep yourself from acting on impulse. Being able to develop from being personally affected by others' remarks to being more objective is not always easy, so if you are still working on this, you can start by immediately diffusing the situation by staying calm and keep yourself from saying something that will stoke the fire. One of the most important skills one needs to master to reach a high level of emotional intelligence is to refrain from acting on impulse. So, step one. Take a deep breath. Take a step back. Evaluate your feelings. Ask yourself if it is necessary to make the situation worse by reacting. Step one is the hardest, so be patient with yourself and practice step one like you would if you don't, for example, want to cause a ruckus like this one at work.

When you are in a social setting with family and friends, focus on participating in discussions that you are in agreement with, even when someone else tries to bring up a negative or non-conducive topic. Trying to win an argument just for the sake of winning is not an example of constructive conversation, and you can diffuse a battle of egos by trying to take the topic in a new direction.

Be polite and, for all you know, the dynamics may change just because of your positive influence. The two actions of loving people and getting along with them can really be as far removed as the North and South Poles.

Chapter 4

Emotional Intelligence at Work

We've arrived at the official hub of EQ—the workplace. After the discovery and development of EQ, its main focus has become leadership in the workplace because it is such a functional tool for achieving success in one's life. Because emotional intelligence is so relevant and integral to interpersonal communication, it is a crucial skill for anyone who would like to achieve success at work. In this chapter, we will once again see, when we apply high EQ decisions versus low EQ reactions, how much they intertwine with the growth mindset versus the fixed mindset and proactivity.

Factors that naturally play a role in one's level of emotional intelligence are personality and a person's upbringing, but this doesn't mean that these skills cannot be acquired and synthetically learned to improve overall achievement and satisfaction in life. A good example is found in a 2011 study focusing on emotional intelligence, showing that individuals who participated in emotional competency training showed not only improvements in these competencies, but that these improvements were also lasting. As a bonus, these participants also showed improved mental well-being and physical health, healthier relationships and social interaction, and decreased levels of cortisol, the stress hormone which secretion should be kept for emergencies (Cherry, 2019).

What's in it for You?

If you are currently looking for a new job or position, it may be useful for you to know that a rescind study indicated 75% of employers would prefer an employee with a high EQ than one with a high IQ (Cherry, 2019). One may wonder if the other 25% of employers may fall within the same industry that requires employees to have a high IQ as a prerequisite, and therefore, they did not choose EQ. Industries like these include the financial industry and some medical fields. Even then though, it is important to have an EQ, so this statistic is very telling. Employers want to hire candidates who are easy to communicate with, who understand things easily, and who don't place their own feelings first unnecessarily.

One of the things that a developed emotional intelligence will help you to do in a mostly stressful workplace is to handle stress more effectively. This includes being able to communicate more efficiently with your coworkers even when you are under a lot of stress yourself. Studies have linked a high EQ with overall job satisfaction, which is not surprising as it seems to affect all aspects of work, including an employee's work performance.

However, many books about emotional intelligence suggest that a high EQ is meant for leaders and top-level managers. However, for the most successful business operations, it is ideal that all workers or employees possess an above-average to high level of emotional intelligence. Once one looks at how someone with a high EQ carries themself in the workplace and compares their behavior with someone who has a lower EQ, the benefits, not only for the business, but for the employee's success, and the reason why an employer would prefer them become evident. Here are a few examples:

While individuals with high EQs aim to solve problems quickly and make intelligent decisions, those with a lower variant choose to hide behind a facade of victimhood, and if there are problems or erroneous actions involved, they will choose to avoid taking responsibility.

As mentioned above, individuals with a high level of emotional intelligence tend to handle stress effectively for themselves and those around them, while someone with a lower score tends to be passive-aggressive, and this quality tends to shine through in the way that they communicate.

High EQ individuals are excellent at sorting out issues between other employees by serving as a source of conflict resolution. One of their qualities that is exceptionally useful here is their high level of empathy. On the other hand, our less capable friends do not like to work as a team and their willingness to cooperate is low.

This being said, don't try to critique the work of someone with a low level of emotional intelligence. They may take it as a personal attack and lash out, and that is a tell-tale sign. Feel free to do so if the person has a high EQ, as they will see it as an opportunity for growth and appreciate the fact that you noticed this for them.

Lift Yourself Up

You don't need to attend an expensive course or EQ seminar if you know what to do and you have the self-determination and patience to develop these skills with sufficient knowledge. Emotional intelligence is now crucial for being successful in the workplace because it is seen as an important component of being a good leader, businessperson, and an employee with potential. Work relationships and business decisions often rest on interpersonal understanding, communication, and teamwork. The best place to start if you want to improve your emotional intelligence in any part of your life is by looking at the quadrants or the original five categories. Some experts tend to think that the original five categories are well-fitted for business, so let's take a look at them and how they translate into healthy functioning within a working environment and what one can learn from them to improve overall well-being, wherever you are in the food chain of employment.

Self Awareness

Self-awareness can help you to navigate some crucial situations in the workplace. If you can practice recognizing your own emotions in an honest and rational way, this will help you to understand your behavior towards others and how you can modify it to play in your favor in crucial situations. However, mastering emotional intelligence is never easy, and we are often in denial about our own emotions and their effects on us and on others. Thus, developing an ability to take a step back and looking objectively at your own emotions and what they mean may take some practice and you may discover that you've been harboring some toxic habits, such as constant denial.

The thing about denial is that it's only you who experiences this outlook on your own feelings and emotions. Those around you look at your emotions objectively, and they can sometimes identify qualities in you that you are hiding from yourself as you are denying yourself what you are actually experiencing emotionally. For example, you may be jealous and choose to express unsubstantiated anger when a fellow employee is promoted instead of yourself. You may not realize that your co-workers can see that your anger is an expression of jealousy, which is not the best way to behave in the workplace. However, if you are in denial of your own emotions, you will not be able to make this connection and you will see your anger as justified. The result could be that you alienate your co-workers as they would view you as unpleasant and as the type of person who doesn't wish anyone else to have success.

Although experiencing jealousy can be inevitable and an individual with a high level of emotional intelligence is not immune to this emotion, they have a more productive way of handling it because they rationally and objectively identify it, see it for what it is, and deal with it accordingly. Instead of allowing emotion to evoke anger, they will try to understand why they are experiencing it and find a solution to overcome the problem. So, if you've never done this before, where would you begin?

1. When you feel an extreme emotion come bubbling up, STOP! Stop the emotion from boiling over or showing, and try to identify it. If you can, seclude yourself and take a deep breath to open your mind. If you are someone who is not in touch with your emotions, you may identify what you are feeling as something different from what it actually is because you haven't yet identified the root cause. An example of this is anger that manifests because of jealousy.

2. In cases like these, the question 'why' is your best friend. Start at the outer layer. Why am I angry? Be honest with yourself. Anger is an emotion that usually manifests as a symptom of a deeper issue. Assess the situation carefully and avoid placing

blame on any outside party while you deconstruct the issue; this is about you and what's going on inside of yourself.

3. The truth might hurt, but if you use it to build yourself up, it's going to make you stronger, wiser, and smarter. So, try to accept the truth. If you can't manage to do this the first time you experience a strong emotion, then be patient with yourself as long as the willingness remains.

Apart from working on being honest about your emotions, you can also focus on looking at the connection between the emotions you experience and the responses that they trigger. Aim to develop an awareness of this as you don't need to wear all of your emotions on your sleeve, especially in the workplace. For example, do the emotions you experience have a big impact on your decisions regarding how you want to or are interacting with your co-workers? By just reflecting, you may start to notice that sometimes, there is decision-making that can be improved or a disconnect that you can start creating between specific emotions and their subsequent decision-making processes due to toxic results.

An additional focus you can add is to take note of your personal emotional strengths and weaknesses, as they will most likely be playing significant roles in the way that you react in situations and in the emotion-to-response process. Recognizing emotional weaknesses is also not always pleasant or easy, especially if someone else puts you on the spot, but it starts with an ability to see them for what they are, and if you can do this without feeling personally attacked, you can move on to develop wisdom about how to use your strengths to your advantage and how to handle and develop your weaknesses to do the same.

Understand the nature of emotions and what they are. Negative emotions, which can cause a lot of damage, are often short-lived by the person who experiences them, but has a lasting effect on the people they are inflicted upon. Know the power of your emotions. By understanding how powerful they are, you can accomplish and reach goals that you may only have dreamed of up until this point. If your co-worker says the same irritating thing they say every day about the way you dress or where you put the stapler on your desk, just smile. Irritation takes up much negative energy and can affect an entire workplace. You don't want to be the one responsible for negative energy, do you?

Self-Regulation

Self-regulation is one of the most important tools used by a successful and happy worker. Business, the sphere within which it functions, and components that affect it like technology, are constantly evolving, and if an employee does not have an ability to self-regulate, they are going to be a nervous wreck or a very bitter and unhappy worker.

Self-regulation can be understood in terms of everything not revolving around you, but the need for you to revolve with it and stay within its motion, even if that requires change. All of us have to do it; the only reason why it looks effortless for some people is that they have developed an ability to self-regulate. There are a few useful techniques you can consider to ease into self-regulation to make it easier to function at work:

1. Think before you react to an announcement or to a sudden commencement of change in your immediate working environment, or a broader environment, that will affect you. The sudden introduction to change may be a shock, but you can make it the least harmful for your own body, mind, and career by first contemplating what it means.

Will this change in your working environment be purely negative or is it your immediate perception of it that makes it seem that way? For example, does this change offer you any hidden opportunities that you haven't considered before? How can you use this situation to your utmost advantage? A great start would be to try and take it in your stride even if others are complaining. Show resilience, and it will be noticed. Show a willingness to adapt, and it will be appreciated and respected.

2. One of the things that makes it really hard to cope with change, especially for the perfectionist types, is that you tend to lose control over the situation to some extent or even completely. This can trigger an emotional overreaction, and a telltale sign of emotional intelligence is the ability to control the panic that flows from the feeling of losing control. Learning to step back and take a breath is not easy, but don't be daunted by this challenge as it is possible to succeed. The way one masters this invaluable skill is by practicing it. Don't be discouraged. Follow the same technique by always keeping in mind that the only things you should worry about controlling are the things that are within the realm of your own control.

3. The final point of focus here is to provide yourself with a form of release that will keep you mentally and physically healthy and help you to maintain a state of calm and control when it feels like things are spinning out of control. Being the face of calm when things go haywire at work will put you a step above the rest when it comes to choosing candidates for responsible positions like management, and you may even find coworkers starting to ask you for advice on personal matters. However, before we go off-topic, think about an activity that can take your mind off of your work, rejuvenate your inner self, and keep your body healthy. If you like taking walks, then do so often. If you enjoy meditating or reading or cooking for your family, enjoy those activities. Keep your body and mind healthy.

Self-regulation is like keeping your body, which is a functioning machine that needs constant care and TLC, well-oiled at the top level and using your mind in the most intelligent way possible so that you can get the most out of life.

Social Skills

Research conducted on emotions and their psychology strongly suggests that individuals who have a high level of emotional intelligence naturally have strong and well-developed social skills. In the workplace, well-developed social skills contribute an overall improvement to the working environment and company culture by leading to more efficient and honest communication and open communication lines where both parties understand each other.

Sure, social skills are important in all life situations and relationships, but in a work setting, they can be that make or break factor regarding your ambitions and goals. Most of us have come across individuals who think that they understand social skills, but kind of miss the target because they see it as an opportunity to see what they can get out of other people while simultaneously trying to stay in everyone's favor. Additionally, if you've witnessed this phenomenon at work, you will also know that succeeding by doing so is virtually impossible and if a person attempts to do it, their understanding of how social networking functions are not linked to a high level of social intelligence. One of the first things that one notices about someone like this is that they talk a lot, but they don't balance out their talking with a lot of listening. There are three key traits that one can focus on to develop the level of social skills that matches someone with a high EQ. They are attainable, but they require an open mind and introspection during the learning process, just as most skills related to high emotional intelligence do. These are the very same factors that we've been talking about from the start. Here are the key focal points that will dramatically improve your social skills plus some tips on how you can practice improving them:

1. Learn to listen earnestly. That means to really listen. Most people listen passively, just waiting until it's their turn to talk while active listeners take in the information presented to them and show this by providing meaningful feedback, indicating that they are paying attention, and asking questions about the information that is communicated to them. The effect that active listening has on the individual who is talking, or perhaps confiding in you, is lightyears apart from that if you were to only passively listen. There is a famous saying that goes *Listen not to respond, but first, to understand.* Active listening cultivates trust between you and the individual with whom you are communicating, and you will be able to build rapport with colleagues

which will improve communication even more. Good leaders are good listeners and team players, all of which require high-level social skills. Active listening also shows that you see the importance of your relationships with your co-workers, you recognize how important healthy relationships affect your job, and that you are able to recognize the bigger picture, which may include the company's goals or mission statement. How does one start to practice active listening? You can start by, while someone is talking to you, making a conscious decision to focus on more than the individual's words. Look at their facial expression, look in their eyes while they are talking, and try to understand what they are telling you with their eyes while you are listening to the words. Put their words into your own words as you follow what they say so that you can understand their words from your own perspective. This will make it easier for you to stay attentive and show the necessary engagement. Finally, be genuine. It's the easiest way to listen actively without forcing yourself.

2. As we referred to looking at the individual's face and eyes of the person with whom you may be communicating in the previous point, so too is

reading body language and nonverbal communication a part of having good social skills. The ability to read another person's nonverbal cues can tell you things about them that they may want to hide, like whether or not they really like you or what their intentions are in a specific situation. Areas of an individual's body that can give you some telling information include their eyes, the posture of their upper body, the way they position their arms and legs when they stand or sit down, and the way that they carry themselves. If you have high emotional intelligence, you will be likely to pick up on these things and use them as a form of reference when you assess your colleagues and the way that they communicate with you and others. For example, do they treat everyone in the same way or do they tend to change their stature depending on who they are communicating with? Effectively reading body language is like having your own personal cheat sheet when it comes to assessing those around you and using the information as a reference to decide how you are going to act or react in a specific situation.

3. Focus on developing functional persuasion skills. Being persuasive can be tricky because one needs to

have an ability to read others accurately. Learning the art of persuasion is part of your EQ toolkit, so we'll be discussing this skill and how to master it in detail later on, as it can be one of the most powerful weapons to use to achieve success in the workplace and in relationships. Keep this one in the back of your mind for now.

4. This last one will not be seen as a skill by everyone, but not only is it a skill, it is an extremely important one. Being drawn into what's going on between co-workers or having short watercooler discussions can blow up in your face and tarnish your reputation as a mature employee with leadership potential. Just don't do it. This includes keeping your own issues private and not discussing them with a 'friend' from work. It's best to have friends outside of work and to keep your work friends separate if you take your career seriously. However, this doesn't prevent you from being proactive and stepping up to solve problems in the office that could prevent harmonious relationships. As long as you practice impartiality and remain fair and honest, doing so can demonstrate your leadership abilities.

Empathy

Having an ability to empathize with others is a core component of having social skills. If you have the ability to empathize, you won't have any trouble putting yourself in someone else's shoes and understanding their situation, whatever it may be. People tend to focus on their own problems and issues, so they don't necessarily acknowledge the value of this ability and how it can ultimately bring individual prosperity and the achievement of life goals. However, empathy does not only mean that you should be able to understand the situations of others, it also involves an intelligent and appropriate response based on that understanding.

There are three main types of empathy; namely, affective empathy, cognitive empathy, and somatic empathy. All three of these are associated with emotional intelligence, but some are more useful than others in the workplace. Before discussing empathy as a singular concept, here are the differences between the types of empathy and what they mean:

- The first type, called affective empathy, involves the ability to specifically understand another individual's feelings and emotions and to use this understanding to respond constructively and appropriately. An example of how affective empathy may manifest is when you understand a situation another person is going through and you develop a feeling of concern for this person's well-being. Look at it this way; if you didn't have affective empathy abilities, you may have known about the person's situation, but would not have developed a subsequent feeling of concern or feel an urge to help. Thus, after identifying emotions in others, you are also able to develop a response that will ultimately help or support the individual and may even improve a bigger picture like the social culture at work.

- Somatic empathy is a bit different. If you experience somatic empathy, you literally experience a physical reaction that is directly linked to what someone else is feeling. For example, when someone else is sad, you may find yourself shedding a tear with them or if they are experiencing a particularly embarrassing moment, your body will react by feeling nauseous or blushing. It's almost as if you are reacting on their behalf. Although this type of empathy is not particularly useful in a workplace context, it is a testament to how connected someone can be to the feelings of others.

- Cognitive empathy is the ability to think about what other people are thinking. This can sound both simple and confusing, so what it means is to actually understand not only another person's thoughts, but also the mental state that accompanied their perspective and what they may be thinking in response to a specific situation. In psychology, this type of empathy relates to what is called the "theory of mind," which is a very useful socio-cognitive skill when it comes to developing an ability to understand others (Cherry, 2020).

When it comes to the workplace, an individual with a high EQ can use their empathic abilities to read co-workers and understand social dynamics between them that others may not be aware of. For example, an empathetic individual may notice that one coworker has a sense of vulnerability which causes them to react in a certain way that is perceived by others to be negative. While this individual is able to understand this, others will not, as they do not see the need nor do they have an awareness to look deeper into the coworker's behavior. For example, you will easily be able to see who is at the head of the office tribe, how behaviors are influenced, and what kind of reactions and interactions originate from these behaviors. This gives you a strategic advantage. Consider the following approaches to empathy and how you can use this multifaceted skill to improve yourself and others in the workplace:

1. Trying to understand someone else's perspective can be difficult because their views will not always agree with yours. This is why someone with a high level of emotional intelligence has the ability to take a step back and not become involved or take things personally. By taking this position from the start, you can avoid a serious conflict situation by resolving the matter while it exists as a less serious disagreement. This quality is great if you need to mediate a situation of conflict, as long as you remove your personal views from the situation.

2. While trying to look at situations from others' perspectives, you can also try to focus on your own response when interacting in situations that require your empathy. Does your response bring about a positive or productive outcome? For example, if two coworkers are in an argument, making them angrier even though you understand both of their perspectives, would not be an example of utilizing

reputable emotional intelligence. Therefore, the way that you use this knowledge to monitor and shape your own behavior and responses is crucial.

Motivation

When we talk about motivation in this context, we are specifically talking about intrinsic motivation. What this means is that you are motivated to reach your goals for yourself and not for any type of external reward or remuneration. This is a dead giveaway for a high EQ. If you could think for a moment, do you know anyone who gets up every morning because they are intrinsically motivated? We are all mostly motivated to go through the daily grind because we have to, we need to make a living to survive, or because we earn a large paycheck that we don't want to give up. However, which part of that is focused on yourself? It's difficult to set goals that are focused on fulfillment when so much of our lives are based on just getting by in a societal framework that we did not choose. It is not impossible, though!

In this world, it is important to make money and other external assets be part of your goals. However, if you have a higher level of emotional intelligence, you realize that these things cannot be injected into your soul to bring happiness. And even if you are not in the ideal space in your life or work at the moment, you can still make the best of it. In fact, making that mind shift may even lead to the type of life you envision for yourself and your family. Having intrinsic motivation will ultimately give you enough grit to push through when you would have otherwise given up on a materialistic goal because it means something to you personally. Are you passionate about what you do? If you aren't yet, then you can still develop a passion that keeps your inner flame going and reaching for success in the workplace. Here are two simple points you can focus on:

1. Find and focus on what you love about your work. Does this sound difficult? If you currently see only the negative or possibly have had a few bad experiences in the past, this is understandably not easy. But what do those with high EQ's do so well? They look on the bright side. And even if there is no bright side yet, they figure out how to make it bright for themselves. A good place to start is by making a list. If there are no good things you can list, which non-good things are possibly changeable, either by changing your perception or by making a more noticeable hands-on change? If you honestly think that there is no way you can start changing either

your perception or to implement more hands-on changes, write down the reasons for this situation. Then, put the notebook you wrote away or save the file you typed and let it rest for a day or two. Keep your choices and thoughts in the back of your mind while you go through the motions for a day or two. Then, revisit your list and see if anything has changed. Do you feel different? Sometimes, we just need to give ourselves time to think or we may be stuck in a mood or between emotional barriers that lift with time. Re-evaluate your choices and also how you are approaching them when you do the exercise for the second time. Is there a difference? Can you initiate a difference in your approach? Finally, do you have the *potential* to initiate a difference in your approach? If you didn't answer yes to the first two questions, you have to answer yes to the third. You do have the potential, and now you know where to start—believing in your own potential.

2. After you've identified what you need to in order to move forward in your EQ journey, keep in mind that motivation requires unwavering positivity. If you found it hard to identify an aspect of your work that you find at least a little bit gratifying, then this

may be a sign that you need to focus on developing a positive mindset. Nothing can be achieved with efficiency, success, and personal gratification if negativity is its driving force. While there may be individuals who know this and understand it by their very nature, it doesn't mean that those who are not like this cannot benefit from this ability. By learning and mindfully putting together the blocks of emotional intelligence, you are showing strength and character as a human being.

Chapter 5

The Powerful Theory of Mind

The theory of mind is a social cognitive skill, but what does that mean? Social cognition is part of social psychology and it focuses specifically on the way that different people absorb, store, and interpret information about other people and social situations that they may find themselves in or are able to observe. So, this social cognitive skill is directly related to the influence that an individual's cognitive processes have on any type of social situation. An interesting aspect of social cognition is how, when defined like this, it can give you an insight into how your mind works, which you can use when you are following thought processes or practicing to become more emotionally intelligent.

The first interesting fact about social cognition is that it doesn't have a singular definition. This may be due to the fact that it's a complex process. However, it can still be understood easily by looking at the following factors:

- Keep in mind that an important component of social cognition involves an individual's perception of others and how they came to know about them.
- Another important component of social cognition is studying an individual's mental processes related to memory, perception, thoughts, and actions directed towards others.
- The final component ties in with the first two by looking at how we process specific information about a social environment, how it is then processed and stored as memories, and then retrieved and used for interpersonal or social interaction.

When looking at these main points, one can see that the brain does a lot of intricate work that we are not aware of to create perceptions, possible preconceptions, and impressions that we use, without thinking twice, to navigate our social environment. Social cognition, which forms the base of the theory of mind, is also applicable to a myriad of different mental processes regarding impressions and mindsets that include prejudice, discrimination, the concept of self, stereotyping, and decision making. It makes sense if you think about it.

The Development of Social Cognition

Social cognition and its development have been observed and studied in people from early childhood and continues through the adolescent years. Children naturally become aware of not only their own feelings, but also of the feelings of others. They also start to understand thoughts and motives in a similar way—both their own and those of others. These abilities open children up to developing prosocial behaviors by learning how to act and respond in different situations and also to take into account the feelings of others. Prosocial behaviors are behaviors that contribute to a positive social context, such as helping others and being courteous. Interestingly enough, in the research of psychologist Jean Piaget, he found that, at an early age, children are predominantly egocentric, which is a trait that is far removed from anything emotionally intelligent. Egocentrism means that a child will only view the world from their own perspective and struggle to see things from the viewpoint of another. This may not occur to them at this early age, except if they are purposefully confronted with the idea, which they may still choose to ignore.

This egocentric behavior changes, however, as a child grows older. This may be due to the fact that a child subconsciously realizes that it is difficult to navigate socially and otherwise if they don't adopt a more sensitive approach to perspective or it may be that they have been taught to do so by their parents or guardians. As Piaget's research and hypothesis are not very recent, new research has emerged in the meantime, indicating that the psychologist's estimation of the link between age and egocentrism may not have been as accurate as previously thought; psychological research has found that children as young as preschool age have a more flexible perspective when it comes to social situations as they are able to understand situations from another individual's point of view. The theory of mind is one of the most important growth components of social cognition that needs to be evident from a young age because it is that underlying ability a person needs to understand the mental states and perspectives of others.

An interesting contributing factor or rather distinguishing factor that affects social cognition is cultural difference. This is because two individuals can develop very different perspectives of similar situations based on their cultural context or background. This brings a sense of variation into an ability that would otherwise have been regarded as more monolithic, but not necessarily simpler, in nature. By the very cultural context that is ingrained in a person's upbringing, two individuals can interpret one situation by experiencing it in opposite ways—one may see it as courteous and the other as rude. Thus, cultural awareness can play an important role in the accurate interpretation of others' perceptions, especially in a multicultural society (Cherry & Susman, 2020).

The Theory of Mind in the Workplace

The theory of mind is the ultimate tool that can help you to understand others. In the workplace, it is crucial to understand others, even if you don't like everyone, as a deeper understanding of each co-worker will help you to understand why people interact with each other in the way that they do and it can also help you to develop a deeper understanding of the larger social context within your workplace. A great way to start developing your own theory of mind if you want to improve its effectiveness is by looking at the five different stages that we go through when we are younger in order to develop a more mature theory of mind. By doing this, you can inspect each stage of development and evaluate your own capabilities in this regard. These five stages occur in our earlier years and they always do so in five stages, sequentially, in a standardized order:

1. Coming to an understanding that the underlying or more evident reasons people may want or desire something can differ for varying reasons.

2. Developing a realization and subsequent understanding that different people do not necessarily feel the same about a particular situation and that they can have different reactions or beliefs about the same thing.

3. Next, coming to truly understand that not all people have an ability to comprehend or believe the truth or that something is or can be true.

4. Realizing and understanding that people may have beliefs about the world that are false or based on false information.

5. The most difficult of the five steps is coming to understand that an individual may have hidden emotions and that they are acting in a way they are not really feeling.

When considering these capabilities, it is crucial to remember that there is a difference between awareness and understanding. If one understands the behaviors of others, it means that one will be able to think about them without judgment instead of reacting emotionally due to being triggered. And, if you think about it, these are human behaviors that are all prevalent in a workplace environment. The thing is, you may be better at understanding some of these abilities, and know that others may require some work, especially if they have a personal link to your own personality or an experience that you've had in the past. For example, if you've had a bad experience with someone who lives their life in complete denial and it had a negative effect on your life or well-being, then understanding this behavior in others may be challenging. That's where emotional intelligence comes in. The ability to separate different situations is what makes one emotionally intelligent, and it will enable you to use the theory of mind to its utmost potential in the working environment.

Other Important Components Linked With the Theory of Mind

To fully understand the theory of mind, there are two sub-components or skills that also require focus. The first is the ability to be introspective and the other is self-awareness. More importantly, to use the theory of mind successfully as an ability and an aid to success in the workplace, these two components not only need to be understood, but one must also understand how they can be developed for the sake of the targeted use of emotional intelligence.

Introspection

The term introspection is also used to describe an exploratory technique that was first developed by psychologist, Wilhelm Wundt. Wundt's technique, also known as *experimental self-observation*, teaches people to carefully and objectively analyze the content of their thoughts.

Some historians have suggested that introspection is not the most accurate term for Wundt's methods. Introspection implies a level of armchair introspection, but the methods Wundt used were a much more controlled and rigid experimental technique (Cherry, 2014).

Introspection is a form of self-awareness and links with two other components that are also related to this part of emotional intelligence. Introspection can be defined as a process of trying to access one's own internal psychological or emotional processes, judgments, states, or perceptions directly. Another method related to introspection is self-reflection. Self-reflection is more about examining, contemplating, and analyzing your own feelings and thoughts, actions, and emotions. Finally, insight is evident when you get a clear idea of a solution to a problem that you are experiencing. Insight is the result of successful and constructive introspection and self-reflection (Nir&Far.com Team, 2019).

Have you ever considered that there may be a right way and a wrong way of practicing introspection? Better adjectives that can be used here are probably constructive and less constructive. If that is true, then what is introspection exactly and how do we know when we're doing it correctly? The purpose of introspection is to look within yourself and perform a type of reflection on a specific emotion, act, or your well-being in general. However, if you want your introspection to mean anything, you need to actively seek answers and not use it as a way to exacerbate your stress levels and worries. An emotionally intelligent way of conducting introspection would involve self-reflection aimed at self-improvement and a raised sense of self-awareness. Another reason to practice introspection is to develop a deeper understanding of yourself and others, and individuals who are naturally introspective tend to maintain stronger relationships, enjoy an increased sense of well-being, and a clearer sense of purpose in life. Practicing healthy introspection can also help you to maintain control of your life by identifying your weaker and stronger points and actively working on them to improve yourself as a human being.

However, thinking about yourself will not automatically result in knowing yourself, so it's important that your introspective efforts lead to insight. There has even been some interesting insight gathered from research that suggests that the more time you spend thinking about yourself, the less insight you are likely to get from it. That's why it's important to do it right and get the results needed for self-improvement. If you want to do constructive introspection, you have to start by following a constructive approach.

The first thing to keep in mind is to not to make introspection an obsessive act. The purpose of introspection is not to nitpick and find fault with yourself;

in fact, if you start doing this as part of your introspective sessions, you could be completely counterproductive. Also, just thinking about yourself all the time is not going to lead to you shouting, “Eureka!” while running naked down the street because you’ve discovered the meaning of life. Individuals who constantly and obsessively do introspection often show signs of anxiety, they have more negative social experiences, and they tend to have low self-esteem. Maybe it’s because their focus is misplaced by looking at their traits or characteristics instead of their actions and choices.

So, what should you do when you’re doing introspection then? It’s not supposed to be a “follow the guide step-by-step” process, but if you are not doing it constructively, it is not going to have the desired effect. So, let’s look at examples of questions you can ask yourself and things you can focus on when you are doing introspection. Many people ask questions that start with ‘why.’ All I can say is, why? By using this simple introductory word, you are programming your brain not to reach too far, but rather go for the most obvious answer. And, the most obvious answer is one that’s most likely based not on objectivity, but on our own pre-existing and subjective beliefs. So, if you look at using the word ‘why’ from that perspective, do you think it’s the most productive approach? To be truly introspective, one needs to be as objective as possible. Don't make yourself miserable by making only answers available that are in your pre-existing framework. There is a reason why asking questions is not the best way to self-reflect, and it actually has a name too. It is a cognitive bias, and it is called *illusory correlation.* Illusory correlation occurs when you ask the 'why' question during introspection and your mind makes connections that appear to be related because of insecurity or another emotion, but from a rational perspective, there is no correlation at all. So, now we have a dilemma. No, we don't! Here's what you can do to get the most from your introspection sessions:

Instead of asking a 'why' question, which is not going to lead you to a constructive answer, you need to ask questions that will help you to focus on the goal or solution you are aiming for. Therefore, you should try asking a 'what' question. For example, you can ask questions like, "What am I feeling at this moment?" instead of, "Why do I feel so awful?" This type of thinking can help you to identify your emotions directly, and this has been shown to reduce negative attitudes and emotions. You can also avoid asking yourself a question that is centered around a problem from the beginning. Don't ask, "What trouble am I facing?" Instead, formulate the question around a goal.

For example, "What do I want my relationship with my wife to be like in two weeks?" Coaches and consultants are discovering that solution-oriented questions make their clients feel better, while problem-oriented questions make their clients feel anxious.

If you have a persistent problem that is bugging you, try approaching the issue by asking yourself questions that shift your focus to a possible solution. It doesn't have to be a complicated phrase. Start by asking yourself, "What is a possible solution to this problem?" and then, "How can I start to move towards creating a solution for what's bothering me?"

Ultimately, there are two benefits to using solution-driven questions:

- They open up and reveal potential answers to problems that could otherwise have stayed hidden.
- This will increase your confidence levels when it comes to solving future issues.

The feeling of taking action and gaining control will affect your sense of confidence, increase your self-esteem, and boost the chances that you will act out the solution and create a positive outcome.

Self-Awareness and Self-Concept

Self-awareness also develops from a young age and is an important component of the theory of mind. Self-awareness means being aware of different aspects of oneself. Examples of these aspects include emotions or feelings, personality traits, and specific behaviors. In its most basic form, it is a psychological state wherein someone becomes their own focus of attention. If you look at this definition, it may seem that we are constantly and consciously focused on these aspects on a daily basis, but the truth is that, even though it is a central aspect of our psychology, we are not constantly focused on it. Instead of being consciously aware of yourself, self-awareness manifests in other ways, like sticking its head out now and then through your personality.

When it comes to the theory of mind, self-awareness intertwines with the concept of self, which is similar. Self-concept is our perception of our abilities, behavior, and what makes us unique; it's like painting a mental picture of yourself. So, with self-awareness, you are experiencing these things, but with self-concept, you have a more concrete and decisive idea of them all put together like a puzzle.

When it comes to self-awareness, there are two different types, which are private self-awareness and public self-awareness. Public self-awareness is when an individual is aware of how they appear to those around them, most likely in a public or social setting. This type of self-awareness makes its appearance when you become the center of attention or when you perform in front of a crowd; for example, when you deliver a speech or do a presentation at work. Because public self-awareness involves other people and society, this type of self-awareness would typically motivate a person to adhere to social norms because they are being observed and evaluated by other members of society. Most people would try to behave in a socially acceptable manner if they know that they are being observed and evaluated by others to avoid criticism.

If a person is not used to public self-awareness or has a negative experience, it can cause anxiety, specifically because they know they are being negatively evaluated. It is this worry about how they are perceived by others that leads to what is called "evaluation anxiety."

Private self-awareness is the other type and involves only you and your perception of yourself. It doesn't involve other people; however, you don't have to be in isolation to experience private self-awareness. An example of private self-awareness is walking down a hall and seeing your reflection in a mirror.

People who become overly self-aware become overly self-conscious, which means that they spend too much time being consciously self-aware. self-consciousness is merely a heightened state of self-awareness; however, it is not a productive way to use one's self-awareness and can also lead to unnecessary stress and anxiety. Ideally, self-awareness should lead to self-understanding, and individuals who fit this description tend to harbor a higher awareness of their own feelings and they are more likely to stick to what they believe in (Cherry, 2014b).

On the other hand, there are two types of self-concept, or rather the ways in which it can manifest. They are congruence and incongruence. An ever-present quality of an emotionally intelligent individual is that they have the ability to look at themselves realistically, and their perception of who they are will rarely be far removed from reality. This definition is in line with a congruent self-concept. Congruence is present when one's self-concept is fairly closely aligned with reality. The term "fairly closely" is used because absolute objectivity is not possible for any human being, and we are all guilty of distorting reality to some degree. Some individuals have the ability to be more realistic, while others develop a self-concept that is incongruent with reality. Thus, congruence, a healthy sense of self-awareness, and correctly applying introspection are parts of nailing the theory of mind (Cherry & Gans, 2013).

Chapter 6

Cultivate Emotional Health in Your Children with Emotional Intelligence

Wanting the best for your child includes wanting them to be emotionally healthy and developmentally able to navigate their world with independence and confidence. You also want your child to attain success, reaching their dreams in life. So, if emotional intelligence is applicable to your life, doesn't that mean that it's also applicable to the life and upbringing of your child? There are two scenarios here. The first is that your child has a naturally high level of emotional intelligence and that you need to learn how to nurture and cultivate this while they develop into adulthood. The second scenario is that your child may be struggling in this department which can affect their social life and academic achievement, to some extent, whereas you can choose to actively set an example for your child to engage them in activities that involve emotional intelligence. Wouldn't you have wanted to acquire this knowledge and those skills when you were a child? It's a fantastic way to give your child a head start in life, and you will notice an improvement in just about every aspect of their development if you mindfully practice an EQ approach with them. Whichever category your child falls into, there is not much of a difference in what you need to do because you are required to adopt the same mindset in both situations. What does this entail? It is very much like practicing improvement of your own EQ, except you would be demonstrating and allowing your child to use or reinforce the techniques themselves while observing.

Your Child's Emotional Needs

Because we spoke about individuals in general earlier, we now know how a child's sense of self and their perceptions of others and others' emotions develop as they get older. From birth, your child starts developing a sense of self and begins to explore the world around them. Babies look at everything wide-eyed and with an unbridled sense of curiosity, and I don't blame them, as there is much to know. In this chapter, however, the focus is on the role that you as a parent play in your child's development of what we call social cognition and the theory of mind. You know the importance of these skills for your child's future, so how can you help your child to develop them from an early age and teach them to apply emotional intelligence to their immediate environment? Your relationship with your child sets a foundation for them to start exploring their environment while feeling safe, supported, and protected. A child's emotional development includes healthy expression and regulation of their emotions, and you are the first person to whom they will look to for reference and guidance. Here are other ways that your child will benefit from parenting with high emotional intelligence.

According to research by the National Academy of Sciences, there are three signs that your child is ready for school. They are a strong motivation to learn, the right intellectual capacity, and a strong emotional or social capacity. The research further found that early strong emotional and social development will lead to future academic success as it is the underlying and key factor that supports all social, emotional, and academic success later in life. An example of how to start developing these skills is by starting to develop a social and emotional relationship with your child from a young age and allowing them to do the same with others.

There are genetic components that can have predetermining effects on a person's social-emotional capacity or EQ, but they do not ultimately shape the ability overall. These components include life experiences, temperament, and unique genetic makeup. The first action that you can take as a parent to start building a healthy emotional capacity for your child is by being as supportive as you can. Here are some examples that will promote the growth of a child's emotional capacity through simple and loving acts:

- Show physical affection towards your child by hugging them, holding them, and kissing them regularly. Talk to them regularly as well, and don't exclude them from all conversations just because they are children.
- Encourage your child to interact with other children in their peer group in a social context. If this can be done from a very young age, it can have positive effects on their social skills later in life. When you are interacting with adults and children in their

presence, model kind, understanding, and generous behavior that they can easily observe.

- Encourage your child to do new things, but do not push too hard if you see that they are genuinely not interested or have no affinity for it. Don't push your child to do something just because you want them to do it; rather, encourage them to explore and make options available for them from which to choose. Show how pleased you are, not only with your child's accomplishments, but also with their efforts.

- Don't hide your own emotions from your child. That being said, overreacting in front of your child or using your emotions incorrectly or impulsively is neither acceptable nor conducive. However, your child needs to know that you have a spectrum of emotional capabilities because you are the first person with whom they are going to start relating on an emotional level. Use your emotions to show your child how to develop a sense of empathy for those around them.

- Create set routines that help your child to feel safe and to promote the ability to develop healthy habits, mentally and physically.

- Always acknowledge your child's emotions and feelings and encourage them to talk about what they are experiencing. When they are upset, react calmly and speak to them in a soft tone. Show them that there is no purpose or reward for overreaction. Finally, comfort your child and show physical affection (La Petite Academy, 2015).

Being an Emotionally Intelligent Parent

For you to teach your child emotional intelligence, you need to practice it yourself on a daily basis. It's actually a great way to keep yourself on track if you are aware that you need to set a consistent example to your children. Because children can be naughty and misbehave, or just be children in general, one of the most challenging skills for parents to master is impulse control. You know, how you feel at a moment when you just want to get the anger and frustration out when your toddler draws a picture with their crayons on the wall for the umpteenth time. When they grow older, their misbehavior can stem from deeper and unaddressed emotional issues, and it is in these situations where not only impulse control, but also empathy, can help you to avoid such actions or reactions from occurring in the future. The aim is to raise an emotionally healthy child and to become or stay an emotionally healthy adult yourself.

Studies have shown that acting without emotional intelligence and giving in to impulses can have a longer-lasting effect than a slap on the bum. Words, and the way that they are communicated, has a phenomenal effect on your child's emotional development, so as a parent, you must practice self-management skills in regard to your own emotions in order to develop a constructive child-raising strategy. When you communicate with your child, they attach the emotion that you show to the words that you are saying, which means that they most likely focus on how the words make them feel, instead of primarily focusing on what the words actually mean. These emotionally-loaded words stay in your child's mind and make a lasting imprint. If your child is used to experiencing angry outbursts and negative language, this can affect the way that they process emotions and their ability to accurately perceive the emotions of others.

Becoming a better and more emotionally intelligent parent starts with managing and regulating your own emotions and emotional responses. Think of the components of EQ like problem-solving, impulse-control, and empathy and how important they are when raising a little living being with a deep developing emotional capacity. It is also important to keep in mind that, if you are co-parenting, keeping a united front is crucial, so these skills should be reflected in both parents' behavior and reactions. It basically comes down to this: If you can't control and prudently use your own emotions, then you can try any parenting strategy available to you and it will not be successful in terms of raising a stable, happy, and emotionally intelligent child.

Firstly, focusing on impulsivity can be difficult because, in some cases, you only realize that you've acted that way afterwards. And, when it's over, it's too late. So, how about thinking of it from a different perspective? For example, when you are talking to a complete stranger, will you just suddenly say something like, "that's really dumb" or if a future potential employer asks you a question in your job interview, would you say "that's a stupid question?" If not, then why suddenly act impulsively when you are with the people you love the most? Surely, they are more important than a complete stranger or a manager at a company. If you think about it, the reason why we're more prone to this type of behavior at home is because that is where we feel the most comfortable and where we feel like we can let loose. However, if you think about it, this is a space that you share with people you love very much, so rethinking your method of letting off steam could be prudent. For example, it's a lot easier to manage your emotions if your stress levels are kept to manageable levels. Find something that you enjoy doing that also enables you to get lower or eliminate those toxic stress levels. Using meditation, learning more about practicing mindfulness, or seeing someone you can talk to are all great ways to reduce toxic impulsive behavior.

Having empathy for others, including your own, can enable you to manage their behavior and help them to develop the ability to do the same. For example, when your child shows that they are upset, even in a dramatic or offensive fashion, first try to understand their point of view before ad-libbing an interpretation that may have a negative effect on them. Ask your child questions about their feelings, as this will help them to develop a way of vocalizing and expressing how they feel in order to cope with and process them in a healthy way. Another approach you can try is to reflect back on whichever emotion your child appears to be experiencing and interacting with them about it. You could say, "you look sad today, Jodie." You can also help your child to see their emotions in context by asking them other questions about how they were feeling earlier, what they were doing, and if something specific happened that caused them to react the way that they did.

As they piece the picture together, you will also get a better idea of what happened and whether your child's emotions typically follow specific patterns.

Developing an ability to accurately understand your child's primary perspective on things, and how they use their emotions accordingly, can help you as a parent to provide accurate guidance and be the most effective parent that you can be. Give your child the attention that they need first while trying to look at the problem from their perspective. Then, after you've made sure that you and your child are on the same page and you understand what's going on inside of their little hearts, you can move on to find a constructive solution.

A constructive solution requires problem-solving skills, and there are different ways to tackle a problem effectively. Here are some guidelines that will keep you on the right problem-solving track:

1. The first, and very important component of problem-solving is actually understanding what the problem is. This is why engaging with your child and being empathetic is crucial and has a very high success rate when applied in problem-solving. It's as simple as this; you can't solve a problem as

effectively as you would want to if you don't understand it's width, breadth, and depth.

2. After you are sure that you understand the problem, keep yourself open to a variety of solutions and options. Even if one solution seems to be the obvious one, this may only be obvious to you. Evaluate your options, consider the needs of your child, and keep in mind all of the information that you have gathered about the situation. How will each solution play itself out? This seems like a long and tedious process, but if you practice it regularly, it will become second nature.

3. Next, after playing trial-and-error in your head, pick a solution that will be a win-win for everyone. Sometimes, you'll find that the only solutions come down to win-lose, lose-win, or lose-lose, but this is more likely to happen if you haven't followed the initial steps of being empathetic and evaluating the situation. Always strive for a constructive, win-win solution that demonstrates fairness and generosity to your child.

4. It's implementation time! If you haven't followed this mindful problem-solving process before, you will have now reached the moment where you will

find out if your trial-and-error estimator is realistic, pessimistic, or a bit idealistic. As long as it's not pessimistic, you're on the right track. Balance is key.

5. The best thing about this mindful approach that involves emotional intelligence is that you can look at each situation in retrospect and evaluate your decision-making skills. This is a brilliant way of fine-tuning your approach and whether you've made improvements in both the EQ and the raising-the-kids departments. For example, is there something you would do differently next time? Did you experience a moment of weakness and lose your cool? Everything is a learning experience if you see it as such. The key is to stay focused and to be determined to improve your and your children's emotional intelligence.

Don't let disappointing moments during your trial and error process let you down when you look at your actions in retrospect. Be positive about the fact that you are actively trying to raise an emotionally and socially healthy child and that you are willing to identify mishaps and learn from them. This is what proactive parenting looks like, and you should be beaming with pride (Stein, 2020).

Raising an Emotionally Intelligent Child

Just like there are ways that you can improve your behavior to help your child to be more emotionally resilient and perceptive, there are also things that you can do to boost your child's emotional intelligence specifically. This goes for children who are naturally emotionally intelligent and also for those who can learn to be so. What we are discussing here is parenting strategies aimed at improving or teaching your child emotional intelligence. All parents would like to see their child become more emotionally and socially aware and intelligent similar to them getting taller with age. Consider these basic practices that can help your child to develop a high emotional and social intelligence which are easily made a part of your everyday life:

1. Be smart with how you express emotions verbally in everyday conversations. The way that you experience and express your emotions as parents becomes a key source of learning material for your child. Babies use natural biofeedback to start learning how to process and express emotions, and this biofeedback comes from you, their parents. There may be days where you experience stress or other negative emotions that are not necessary for

your child to experience. The reason for this is because the source of this stress, which can be something work-related, most likely has nothing to do with your child, so exposing them to these emotions can cause an unnecessary mirror effect. If you feel this happening, just take a step back, take a deep breath, and find your center. Don't let your child sense the negativity; rather, focus on expressing uplifting and positive emotions in your conversations. However, if you are in a situation where you are obviously flustered and your child can see this, it can be constructive to discuss what you're experiencing with your child instead of leaving them in the dark or taking away their sense of security. For example, engage with your child by saying, "Lucy, do you see how Daddy is breathing faster and how my body is moving quicker than usual? This is because I forgot to do something at work yesterday, and I don't want to disappoint anyone there." You can continue by telling your child that it has nothing to do with them, so they don't need to feel bad—you're going to fix it when you get to work. Your child will benefit greatly from this, as understanding what's going on in contrast to prolonged uncertainty can help them to feel safe and secure, and will aid in them having an ability to focus their attention on experiencing a healthy childhood.

2. Research has found that individuals who tend to read literary fiction have a larger capacity for developing intellectual empathy. Intellectual empathy is the ability to understand the inner motivations and feelings of others on a high level. You don't have to wait until your child is able to read full-length fiction novels to use this; start cultivating your child's intellectual empathy by reading bedtime stories to them that focus on the feelings, thoughts, and social interaction between its characters. As you move through the story, ask your child questions about what you are reading and about the emotions that you are describing in the story to see how they perceive them. Some emotions or actions in the story may make your child angry; for example, if one character lies to another. Ask them why they feel this way. By reading your child's fictional bedtime stories, you will not only develop your child's capacity to understand the emotions of others, but you will also get to know your child a bit better every night.

3. Even though you are there to protect your child and give them a hug when they are sad, this will not be the case forever. You can proactively prepare your child to live an emotionally intelligent life by teaching them healthy coping mechanisms and teaching them to "self-soothe." If you think about it, teaching a child healthy coping mechanisms from an early age can most likely help them to stay away from turning to unhealthy ones, like substance abuse, when they're older. To achieve this, the first thing we as parents need to understand is that a child experiences emotions very intensely, and their ability to control their impulses is not yet fully developed. This is why children overreact so often; their feelings may seem too big to handle at that specific moment. Actively helping your child to regulate their reactions and the way in which they process them will bring them great advantages in life. The only thing that's important to know is that this process can take time and it may test your ability to control and regulate your own emotions as a parent.

   If your child is still very young, the best place to start is by helping your child to identify what they are feeling when they experience intense emotions.

Try initiating a conversation about their emotions to help them become aware of them and develop the ability to identify them. For example, "I see that you look sad now that your soccer practice is over. Do you feel like this because you enjoyed it so much?" Go along with your child's reaction and help them to find a way to cope. For example, "You're going to soccer practice again next week, so let's see what can make you happy in the meantime." An example of what not to do is to say "don't cry." What you are essentially saying to your child if you say that is that you are too uncomfortable to help them deal with their emotions. Instead, say "don't be ashamed to cry, I'll be here with you until you feel better."

4. The best way to get the gist of your child's emotional capacities in different settings is to observe their behavior. Keep an eye out for how your child decides to interact with their peers as this is a crucial skill that not only develops into a multi-faceted concept as one becomes more emotionally mature, but also serves as an indication of your child's potential success in life. It's important to teach your child how to be a good friend to others and what this means. Observing your child's behavior in social settings can provide you with

important clues regarding their social or emotional strong points and also important clues regarding the social abilities that may require more attention. It may be that they show signs of lacking self-regulation skills by only wanting to do certain activities, but being stubbornly defiant when it comes to other ones. There can be several reasons why your child wants to stick to doing one activity. For example, they may experience other activities as intimidating or difficult, so they are reluctant to try them out. As a parent, you can provide guidance by showcasing your own ability to self-regulate and by also working more closely with your child, and interacting with them, and providing them with support and the guidance that they need to overcome the reason why they are unwilling to adapt. Tools to gently help your child adapt include using their hobbies, talents, including games and toys, helping with the family chores, and partaking in family activities (Vigliotti, 2019).

Chapter 7

Attaining Emotional Intelligence in a Nutshell: Your Go-To Practice Chapter

If you've reached this point, you've consumed, chewed, and digested a lot of information. This last chapter is your toolbox; an easy go-to that provides basic focal points that you can refer to if you don't want to go into detail every time you practice improving your emotional intelligence. You can do them in whichever way you like; by doing one a day, one a week, or more. It's up to you.

1. **Start becoming more aware of how you feel and practice it regularly.**

   We lead hectic, stressful lives and it is all too easy, and in the moment even convenient, for us to neglect our emotions. Try setting a reminder for various points throughout the day to reconnect. When the timer goes off, take a few deep breaths and notice how you are feeling emotionally. Pay attention to the area where the emotion manifests itself physically in your body and how you feel. The more you practice, the more it will become natural and habitual for you.

2. **Always question your own thoughts and opinions as you would question someone else's.**

   In a world where everyone and everything is connected, it's easy to create an opinion bubble around yourself, which occurs when your opinions are constantly reinforced and supported by others who hold the same views. You need to question your opinions even if you still think that they are right or true. This will open you up to understanding other people and you will be more open to new ideas in general.

3. **Always be aware of your own behavior.**

Take time to also notice your behavior as you practice your emotional awareness. Pay attention to how you react or behave when you experience specific emotions and how this influences your daily life. Managing your emotions becomes easier once we become more aware of how we react to them.

4. **Learn to take responsibility for your feelings.**

You cannot blame anyone else but yourself for your own behavior. You are the only person who can control yourself and who can make your choices. Always remember that.

5. **Find a balance between the positive and the negative by learning from the negative and celebrating the positive.**

Emotional intelligence is a key part of celebrating and reflecting on the positive moments that we experience. People who experience positive emotions are more resilient and are more likely to have happy relationships, which helps them to overcome difficult times in their lives. At the same time, learn from the negative, and discard that which is not of any use. This will also make you stronger and emotionally resilient.

6. **Try to be as objective about yourself as you can in all situations.**

It is difficult to know yourself completely and it is almost impossible to look at yourself objectively. Hence, it is important that you reach out to those who know you. Ask them what your strengths and weaknesses are, take note of what they tell you, and compare the information. Look for patterns and remember to not argue with them. It's not about being right or wrong; it's about them helping you to gauge your perception from another point of view.

7. **Identify and understand what motivates you in your life.**

Everyone has something that motivates them when they start a new project or venture in life. The difficult part is clinging to your motivation in the face of adversity. It often happens that people start a project, but don't finish it, because they lose their motivation along the way. Take time to figure out and understand what motivates you intrinsically, and use it to push yourself toward achievement.

8. **Identify and acknowledge the things that trigger you emotionally.**

Individuals with a strong sense of self-awareness have the ability to identify their emotions as they experience them. It is crucial to be flexible with your emotions and to have a sense of adaptability for different situations in which you may find yourself. Avoid denying your emotions, but also avoid being over-critical. The best approach is to give yourself time to process your emotions before acting on them.

9. **Get out your diary and maintain a schedule.**

Making sure that you create a schedule and stick to it is extremely important if you want to accomplish tasks consistently and effectively. Tell yourself (and document it) what you're going to do, how/where you're going to do it, and how long it's going to take you.

10. Live healthfully.

This goes without saying. A healthy body equals a healthy mind. There are different opinions about how to stay healthy and some individuals like to take health to the extreme. Keeping your stress levels down and eating your greens sounds like a good starter plan.

11. Control your anger.

Turn your emotional energy or anger into something more useful. It's okay to keep overwhelming emotions inside temporarily (sometimes it's necessary), especially when the time isn't right to let them out. However, you don't have to spend all that energy on expressing pointless anger. If I were you, I'd turn the anger into motivation.

12. Have personal, intrinsic goals.

Personal goals can provide short-term motivation and long-term direction. So, think about where you want to be and what you want to achieve as an individual, and set some goals for yourself. Build your goals on your strengths and make them relevant to your life. You can even make them fun, which will make them more achievable. Just make sure that your goals are realistic. I hope you are feeling motivated!

13. **Practice positivity and strive to have a growth mindset.**

To stay motivated, it is important to maintain a positive and optimistic mindset. Consider problems and setbacks as learning opportunities instead of failures. Avoid negative people and choose to surround yourself with positive and well-motivated people—they will have a great effect on you.

14. **Repeat after me: The magic happens outside of my comfort zone!**

3...2...1...self-regulation starts NOW! The biggest obstacle to realizing your full potential is not challenging yourself often enough. Great things can happen to you if you're willing to leave your comfort zone, so do it as often as you can. See change as a positive in your life and take from it that which will enhance your life. You can help others to deal with change if you understand that change isn't always bad.

15. Remember that listening is a multi-componential skill.

Before you are able to empathize with someone, you must first put yourself in their shoes by listening to what they are saying and viewing their situation from their perspective. Remember that active listening is the only way to truly understand what another individual is telling you. Listening is the epicenter of empathy—it means allowing the person to talk without any interruption, not developing any preconceptions, and actively trying to understand the issue. Allow yourself to absorb their situation and consider how they may be feeling before you decide how to react.

16. Perspective is everything, so keep it healthy.

We all know the phrase "put yourself in their shoes" and this is exactly what perspective is all about. The easiest way to get a little perspective the next time a problem or situation arises is to switch places with the other person and really think about what is happening from their point of view. Sometimes, there is no right or wrong and only a grey area can be observed, but at least you will understand enough to come to a solution, compromise, or provide some useful advice.

17. **Start working on those social skills.**

    A great way to start improving your social skills is to first identify and then isolate a skill that you know needs some development. By following this approach, you can narrow down the task to give it more focus. Why don't you find an 'idol;' someone you know who is good at that particular social skill, and observe how they act and how they control their emotions. You can then use the observations as a guideline for implementing and applying that skill to yourself.

18. **This is just a reminder, created especially for you, to tell you that practice can make you go places. To master a skill, you need to practice, practice, practice and then practice it some more.**

Practice makes perfect
You can do it!

19. Get away from social media every once in a while.

I don't mean to sound naggy, but taking your social life offline and engaging with people face to face will sharpen your social skills and open up many opportunities to acquire and develop your emotional intelligence. Instead of sending your insufferable aunt an emoji, meet her for coffee as a challenge. Emotional intelligence cannot be properly practiced or improved on social media or online.

20. Pay attention to non-verbal communication.

Remember that nonverbal communication goes both ways. So, when you are reading someone else's body language, they may be doing the same with you. They may not be as informed as you are, though. However, the thing about nonverbal communication is that it has a subconscious effect. Something to remember here is that tonality or the tone of someone's voice is a form of nonverbal communication. Another crucial thing to remember is that a person's body language should be looked at in the context it was observed in, and not in an isolated fashion. You can achieve a lot with positive and confident body language, so make sure to become an expert in this department.

21. Avoid the drama.

People with a high level of emotional intelligence offer good advice, they listen actively, and they empathize with those in need, but they do not allow the lives and emotions of others to affect or rule theirs. If there's drama, don't let it get to you.

22. Avoid those complainers (and if you are one, quit it)!

If someone complains, it means two things; one, that they are victims, and two, that there are no solutions to their problems, which is almost never the case. Complaining is a way to avoid accountability and to look for someone or something to blame. Individuals with a high EQ think constructively and are proactively looking to solve problems.

23. Don't be so critical.

Nothing destroys a person's morale and self-esteem faster than being overly critical towards themselves or towards someone else. Remember that people are only human and most likely have the same emotions and insecurities as you do. Instead of being overly critical, take time to understand another person, and then communicate the change that you want to see.

24. **You are now officially a curious human being.**

People with a high level of empathy have a quenchless curiosity about strangers, their habits, their thoughts, and their feelings. When we talk to people outside of our normal social circle, we can learn much by attempting to recognize and begin to understand opinions, attitudes, and lives that are different from our own. By being curious, you expand your emotional soundboard which enables you to reach high levels of understanding and empathy because you understand human beings much better (RocheMartin, 2019).

25. **Just a final reminder that you're in this for the long haul.**

It's important to understand emotional intelligence for what it is—an endless opportunity for learning. No matter how experienced you think you are in the

EQ department, there will be days where life surprises you and you need to take a humble step back to admire your own mind and the minds of others. These pointers are for you to plant the seeds; what we want are big, evergreen trees of knowledge and understanding to start growing. Allow them to grow by respecting the power of the human mind and how much happiness it can bring.

Conclusion

The one thing that I will always find to be astounding is the fact that something can happen in the human brain in a split second, but that it takes several pages of writing to explain the process. Emotional intelligence surely is the intelligence of the future as it not only creates one healthy human being, but it spreads its positivity when applied in a group format and when there is just one person present who sets an example.

It is important to remember that developing emotional intelligence starts with small steps. It is absolutely imperative for anyone who wants to undertake this rewarding journey to avoid abandoning the quest when they experience negativity, failure, or resistance.

When you look at how to use emotional intelligence in a family context, for example, it's easy to see that the cooperation between partners is crucial, so if this agreement doesn't exist, there need to be other measures taken. Emotional intelligence, unlike cognitive intelligence, is applicable to all aspects of life, and it also has the ability to improve all aspects of life, which can enable the improvement of cognitive intelligence.

At first, it seems complicated when emotional intelligence is divided into five components and then into four. And while reading, you may have been amazed at how much detail there was under each point. However, after you've gone through all of the information and you can take a step back and look at the bigger picture, you will notice that all of the subpoints are like little veins that connect to a larger vein which, in turn, connects to an artery. You would start to see that the smaller components are there to help you to understand the bigger ones and that, once you understand them, you can start focusing on larger points in the development of your emotional intelligence. So, it may seem daunting at first, but one develops a collective understanding of all of the subcomponents that are involved in emotional intelligence.

Take a moment to think about all of the information that you've just taken in; it is vast. And these are fleeting moments of processing that occur in our minds. This is where the final chapter comes in. It is your starter kit to improve your emotional intelligence. These points serve as a reminder, source of inspiration, or daily task; whatever you want them to be. They provide you with a more condensed form of guidance which allows you to know where you can start the development process.

May you gain from these skills what you've envisioned from the start and gain immeasurable wisdom and happiness by understanding yourself and understanding others.

References

Accipio. (2018). *Goleman's 5 elements of EQ*. Accipio.com. https://www.accipio.com/eleadership/mod/wiki/view.php?id=1835

Bisignano, A. (2018, May 29). *Making love last: The Importance of emotional intelligence*. GoodTherapy.org Therapy Blog. https://www.goodtherapy.org/blog/making-love-last-importance-of-emotional-intelligence-0601184

Boniwell, I. (2008, November 7). *Positive emotions and emotional intelligence: The positive impact of negative emotions.* PositivePsychology.org.Uk. http://positivepsychology.org.uk/your-emotions-and-you/

Cherry, K. (2014a, January 6). *A look at introspection.* Verywell Mind; Verywellmind. https://www.verywellmind.com/what-is-introspection-2795252

Cherry, K. (2014b, January 17). *What is self-awareness?* Verywell Mind; Verywellmind. https://www.verywellmind.com/what-is-self-awareness-2795023

Cherry, K. (2019). *5 ways to become more emotionally intelligent at work.* Verywell Mind. https://www.verywellmind.com/utilizing-emotional-intelligence-in-the-workplace-4164713

Cherry, K. (2020, May 2). *What is empathy?* Verywell Mind.

https://www.verywellmind.com/what-is-empathy-2795562

Cherry, K., & Gans, S. (2013). *What is self-concept and how does it form?* Verywell Mind. https://www.verywellmind.com/what-is-self-concept-2795865

Cherry, K., & Gans, S. (2019, September 29). *Why the theory of mind is important for social relationships.* Verywell Mind. https://www.verywellmind.com/theory-of-mind-4176826

Cherry, K., & Susman, D. (2020, May 30). *Social cognition and the world around us.* Verywell Mind. https://www.verywellmind.com/social-cognition-2795912

Counselling Connection. (2016, August 12). *Emotional intelligence: Definition and a brief history.* Counselling Connection. https://www.counsellingconnection.com/index.ph

p/2016/08/12/emotional-intelligence-definition-and-a-brief-history/

Deutschendorf, H. (2019, February 8). *7 ways to gauge emotional intelligence through body language.* Fast Company; Fast Company. https://www.fastcompany.com/90300207/7-ways-to-gauge-emotional-intelligence-through-body-language

Eurich, T. (2017, June 2). *The right way to be introspective (yes, there's a wrong way).* Ideas.Ted.com; ideas.ted.com. https://ideas.ted.com/the-right-way-to-be-introspective-yes-theres-a-wrong-way/

Ewers, P. (2017, January 19). *The definitive guide to understanding proactivity and becoming a proactive entrepreneur.* Mindmaven.com. https://mindmaven.com/blog/proactivity/

Fletcher, J. (2015, July 30). *The important connection between body language and EQ.*

Www.Linkedin.com. https://www.linkedin.com/pulse/important-connection-between-body-language-eq-joan-fletcher

La Petite Academy. (2015, February 27). *Promoting social-emotional development in your child.* Lapetite.com. https://www.lapetite.com/blog/2015/02/promoting-social-emotional-development-in-your-child/

Maria Conceição Serra. (2016, August 26). *People for success.* People for Success. http://p4s.pt/en/the-4-pillars-of-emotional-intelligence-and-why-they-matter/

Mindset Works. (2017). *The growth mindset - what is growth mindset - mindset works.* Www.Mindsetworks.com. https://www.mindsetworks.com/science/#:~:text=Dweck%20coined%20the%20terms%20fixed

Nir&Far.com Team. (2019, May 7). *Here are the 4 simple introspection steps that will boost self awareness.* Nir and Far. https://www.nirandfar.com/introspection/

Palmer, B. (2018, May 22). *Growth mindset and emotional intelligence.* Genos International. https://www.genosinternational.com/growth-mindset/

Practical Emotional Intelligence. (2013a). *History-of-EQ.* Emotional-Intelligence. https://www.emotionalintelligencecourse.com/history-of-eq/#:~:text=Peter%20Salovey%20and%20John%20D

Practical Emotional Intelligence. (2013b). *Increase-your-eq.* Emotional-Intelligence. https://www.emotionalintelligencecourse.com/increase-your-eq/

Riopel, L. (2019, March 12). *Emotional intelligence frameworks, charts, diagrams & graphs.* PositivePsychology.com. https://positivepsychology.com/emotional-intelligence-frameworks/

RocheMartin. (2019). *50 tips for improving your emotional intelligence.* Rochemartin.com. https://www.rochemartin.com/blog/50-tips-improving-emotional-intelligence/

Sáez, F. (2020). *The importance of being proactive.* Facilethings.com. https://facilethings.com/blog/en/proactivity

Skills You Need. (2011). *Social skills in emotional intelligence | skillsyouneed.* Skillsyouneed.com. https://www.skillsyouneed.com/ips/social-skills-emotional-intelligence.html

Stareva, I. (2016, April 4). *The 4 key emotional intelligence capabilities [infographic].* Www.Iliyanastareva.com.

https://www.iliyanastareva.com/blog/4-key-emotional-intelligence-capabilities-infographic

Stein, S. J. (2020). *How to be an emotionally intelligent parent*. Dummies. https://www.dummies.com/health/mental-health/how-to-be-an-emotionally-intelligent-parent/

Vader, K. (2019, August 12). *Emotional intelligence in love and relationships - HelpGuide.org*. Https://Www.Helpguide.org. https://www.helpguide.org/articles/mental-health/emotional-intelligence-love-relationships.htm

Vigliotti, A. (2019, September 30). *Parenting for emotional intelligence*. Psychology Today. https://www.psychologytoday.com/za/blog/the-now/201909/parenting-emotional-intelligence

www.ingramcontent.com/pod-product-compliance
Lightning Source LLC
LaVergne TN
LVHW010059110826
845155LV00028B/415

* 9 7 8 1 9 5 5 0 7 8 0 0 9 *